BOOKS
THAT MADE THE
DIFFERENCE

BOOKS
THAT MADE THE
DIFFERENCE

WHAT PEOPLE TOLD US

Gordon and Patricia Sabine

With a Foreword by
DANIEL J. BOORSTIN

LIBRARY PROFESSIONAL PUBLICATIONS

CONTENTS

APPENDIX

FOREWORD

The members of the Book-of-the-Month Club—and they have numbered millions over the years—are people who believe that "Books Make the Difference." By building family libraries of good books, book clubs have been a great silent force in American education. What other American institution, outside of our schools and libraries, has done more to promote the habits of book-buying and book-reading, and the love of books? Who can count all those who have been awakened to the varied delights of books by the shelf of book-club selections at home, and by the sight and memory of their parents, sisters, and brothers enjoying those books?

The Center for the Book in the Library of Congress, founded by law in 1977, also has been promoting the fellowship of books. Funded by private contributions from individuals and corporations, the Center aims to see that books do not go unread, that they are not lost by neglect nor drowned by specious alternatives or synthetic substitutes. The Center also aims to spur the diffusion of books across our country and around the world, and to use all technologies to promote books and their reading. For example, for five years the "Read More About It" project, co-sponsored with the CBS Television Network, has brought performers to the screen to suggest books for enjoyable follow-up reading after their featured programs. "Read More About It" suggestions are also heard on CBS Radio. The Center aims to remind us that Books Make the Difference to our nation as well as to individuals.

The "Books That Made the Difference" project, begun and sponsored by The Center for the Book, brings you in this brief volume the answers of the widest assortment of Americans to the questions "What book made the greatest difference in your life? What difference did it make?" Here, in their own words, are respondents' answers selected from 1,382 interviews. The answers are not only fun to read but are often surprising and inspiring. They show us the wonderfully varied power of books, and remind us of some neglected classics and other works that we may want to take into our own lives. People across the country are setting up their own Books Make the Difference projects in their towns or neighborhoods. To learn more about this or other activities of The Center for the Book, write to Dr. John Y. Cole, Executive Director, The Center for the Book, The Library of Congress, Washington, D.C. 20540.

Daniel J. Boorstin
The Librarian of Congress

PREFACE

"Let's get married," he said to her, "and then let's take off a year. We can get acquainted and also seek out beauty wherever it is in the world."

They agreed. But then came along the *Books That Made the Difference* project.

The assignment for this *Books That Made the Difference* study came from The Center for the Book, which is the Library of Congress program that promotes books and reading—and does it with private funds, not tax dollars.

She'd been teaching journalism and doing her own writing and editing at Ohio State University. He'd been teaching journalism and doing his own writing at Virginia Tech. Long before, each had begun as a newspaper reporter.

The Sabines became better acquainted, all right, and indeed found beauty in many settings. They simply could not refuse a project dealing with books, so they spent much of the year roaming the United States, she pointing the camera, he the microphone, finding 1,382 interesting Americans and asking:

"What book made the greatest difference in your life?" and "What was that difference?"

The assignment, of course, basically was a reporting one. The first trick was to find those interesting Americans—not chosen by computer, not fitting pre-determined demographics, not constituting a scientifically valid sample of the nation. But interesting because of who they were, what they'd done, where they worked, sometimes even how they looked or precisely where we found them.

The next trick was getting them to say something. Sometimes we interviewed twenty persons in a day, sometimes thirty, sometimes only five. We listened hard and tried to stay tuned in until the interviewee went beyond platitudes. Then we trimmed nearly fourteen hundred interviews to two hundred for the book.

We interviewed in two dozen major American cities and another two dozen smaller ones across the country. We recorded each subject telling us about the book that had made the greatest difference in his or her life. We listened to about one thousand persons face to face, telephoned another one hundred, and read 302 letters Susan Stamberg generated with her program, "All Things Considered," on National Public Radio. We heard from residents of all states except a half dozen of the smallest.

What we went after was the human story, not the statistic. The account of the change caused by the book was more revealing than the title of the book that caused it.

A study just like this—with exactly the questions we asked— never had been done before.

We feel privileged for the experience. So many people shared so much of themselves, told so intimately about themselves—and not always favorably. The questions got to them, went beneath the surface, sometimes painfully, many times with such joy that they just wanted to talk on and on and on.

Which, of course, was part of the beauty we found.

Many persons helped. What these people did was very special:

Ann Heidbreder Eastman, coordinator for the project that produced this book and also director of public affairs programs, College of Arts and Sciences, Virginia Polytechnic Institute and State University.

Larry Besant, director, the Linda Hall Scientific-Technical Library, Kansas City, Missouri.

Dr. Lester Asheim, distinguished professor of library science, University of North Carolina, Chapel Hill.

Dr. John Y. Cole, director, The Center for the Book.

And all the resourceful reference librarians at both Ohio State and Virginia Tech.

INTERVIEWS
FROM THE NATIONAL
BOOKS THAT MADE THE DIFFERENCE
PROJECT

HOW MUCH DIFFERENCE
DO BOOKS REALLY MAKE?

That books do make a difference in people's lives was no surprise to us. That people would unhesitatingly reach so deep to share those differences we did not expect. For example:

A young man in his twenties heard about our project. He wrote that his book was *Life After Life* by Raymond A. Moody, a collection of interviews with people who have survived bodily death and who believe the soul lives on after death.

"It came when my wife and I were splitting, and what I really was doing was finishing up details, so my suicide would be swift and clean.

"I never thought that religion was for me, but when I read this, it changed things immediately.

"I wanted to live."

———

Neither did we anticipate the wide range of impact that books had made:

A man named a book that helped him develop a healthier lifestyle after his heart attack.

A book comforted a man grieving after his mother's death.

A book bolstered a minister's moral strength.

A book saved a lawyer's sanity and preserved his career.

A book inspired a young man to become an actor.

A book helped a woman be more receptive to love.

Books led two people to find mates.

A book helped dissolve a racial color line.

Books changed one man's politics and salvaged another from alcoholism.

A book guided a young mother away from whipping and hollering to talking it out.

Here's what they had to say:

Paul Ouellette had been a silversmith and sometime candlestick

3

maker for Reed and Barton in Taunton, Massachusetts for forty years. Recovering from a heart attack, he found *The Power of Positive Thinking* by Norman Vincent Peale, a guide to a new self-confident pattern for life.

"Before that, I don't know whether it was the stress or what, but I wasn't too sure of myself. I'm a high school dropout competing with graduates, and I just didn't have all the confidence I needed.

"When you're recuperating from a heart attack, time hangs heavy on your hands. There are just so many crossword puzzles you can do, just so many newspapers you can read, and I had gotten sick of reading fiction.

"So I picked this book up just for a lark, you might say, and it really changed my way of thinking. It has helped me learn how to live a different life, really. It used to be I was always on the go: hurry, hurry, do this, do that. Now I've learned how to relax due to this book. There have been no more heart attacks."

———

Sometimes the difference was a healthier way to live.

A caller to our radio program on WRNG, Atlanta said *The Prophet* by Kahlil Gibran, musings by the poet-mystic.

"It made what I had thought were great mountains of worry into molehills. It helped me be more honest and look at things with reason and logic and reality rather than pure emotion and selfishness. It helped me not to feel guilty, to get rid of people and things and thoughts that were garbage in my life."

And another named *The Keys of the Kingdom* by A. J. Cronin, the life story of a lovable Scottish priest.

"I read it when my mother was dying of cancer. It gave me the comfort I needed."

———

Actor Walter Matthau was on location when we tried to reach him.

His agent said he was at the Watergate hotel in Washington, getting ready to shoot two weeks of a motion picture. He suggested we write instead of telephone. We did, and the director of the Center for the Book handed the letter to the desk clerk at the Watergate. The answer came back the same way. (See page 5.)

The Secret in the Daisy is about a sixteen-year-old's gropings for love and security.

———

WALTER MATTHAU

November 4, 1980

Mr. Gordon A. Sabine
c/o The Center for the Book
The Library of Congress
Washington, D.C. 20540

Dear Mr. Sabine:

The book that made the greatest
difference in my life was "THE
SECRET IN THE DAISY," by Carol Grace,
Random House, published 1955.

The difference it made was
enormous. It took me from a
miserable, unhappy wretch to a joyful, glad-to-be-alive human. I
fell so in love with the book that
I searched out and married the
girl who wrote it.

Most sincerely,

WM/g

5

Sometimes the difference is getting control of your life.

Alcoholics Anonymous requires its members to attend meetings and also to read its "big book," the story of the way that many men and women have recovered from alcoholism. A caller to the San Francisco radio station boomed out, "the Alcoholics Anonymous book made the greatest difference for me.

"I started waking up in dry beds, not in jail, and not wondering which jail and what town and what for."

Marcus Cohn was well on his way to earning his first million dollars. The firm of lawyers he headed in Washington, D.C. was the country's largest specializing in broadcast and media law.

He worked weekdays and weekends. Early in the morning, until midnight if necessary. He took work home; he took it with him on vacations.

The son of Russian immigrants, he knew his goal: prestige, power, money. Always more clients, more success, more money.

But something was missing. He felt like a slave to his profession. He hardly knew his children. He and his wife had almost no social life. He became restless, asking, "Is that all there is to life?"

Then, in the early 1960s, a book came to his rescue.

"It literally saved my sanity," he remembers. "It told me who I was and what my problem was. It told me how to start living again. I read the first chapter and said to myself, 'My God, he's writing about me.' Then I never put the book down, I didn't even eat, until I finished it."

It was by Erich Fromm, the famous Austrian psychologist and the first of some two dozen books. He'd just fled Hitler's Europe for the United States, and some of that experience was reflected in both the title and the subject: *Escape From Freedom.*

The book says that freedom—from oppressive rulers or from poverty—can be both good and bad.

All too often, it's a trap. We can't decide exactly what we want to do in life, so we borrow ready-made goals from someone else. Then we become slaves to that way of life, which makes us into automatons just like all the other automatons.

And we become weak and afraid—and slip back into bondage, or slavery, again.

"I surely fit that pattern," Cohn declares. "I lived, ate, and breathed that law firm. I lived a vertical life—always up, up, up the ladder.

"Then Erich Fromm became my therapist. It was as though I were sitting at his feet, having a personal dialogue with him. He turned my life around."

Cohn cut back to a normal work week. He spent more time with a hobby, the theatre. He took his son for a month's sightseeing through the southern United States. He dazzled his young daughter with a weekend in New York City, a plush suite at a fancy hotel, dancing, seeing the sights.

"The kids must have been saying, 'This isn't the same old Dad we used to know,' " Cohn chuckles. "About all I'd done before was kiss them goodnight."

He put in a pool and learned to swim. When he was sixty, he learned to water-ski. He and his wife drove around Italy for a month, so totally unscheduled his office couldn't reach him. And he took off a week or two every year to attend seminars at the Aspen Institute for Humanistic Studies on subjects far removed from either law or broadcasting.

This made him a better lawyer, he's convinced.

"As I do more thinking outside the strict structures of the law, I'm able to bring back to the office more intelligence, more background. I'm more sensitive and more involved with the rest of the world. I've exposed myself more to other people's thoughts."

Through all his longer and longer absences, the firm has continued to succeed. And even his attitude toward money has changed.

"I realized that once one has security, money is inconsequential. Oh, sure, there's a certain amount of ego satisfaction in making more money. But that raises the question of whether making money is the beginning and ending of life.

"Unfortunately, too many lawyers, too many persons in all professions, too many persons everywhere, are completely dedicated to just that one thing. That makes them slaves.

"What they need is what I needed—an escape from their own kind of freedom. They ought to read that book."

———

Another of Fromm's books made the difference to Mary Langan, editor and writer, Fairbanks, Alaska:

"I went to a convent school and heard a lot about Christian love but never really understood what it meant until I read Erich Fromm's *The Art of Loving*. Frankly, we didn't get a lot of love from the nuns. There was a lot of rivalry between the girls and them, and it was hard to love someone you didn't like.

"But Fromm explained love more as sympathy with their view, understanding where they came from and their feelings. I learned that love was sort of walking in the other person's moccasins and seeing how you might have been that way, too, if you'd had their background.

"I was brought up to believe you had to save yourself for a man, be a virgin, go into marriage pure, and then you'd have a beautiful life. But Fromm said you can't start loving somebody all of a sudden; love is something you develop. You get along with other people. It's a skill, an art to be developed.

"When I started living that way, I had a lot better relationship with people. I stopped being so afraid of a love relationship with a man. Before, I was trying to save myself for Prince Charming. I waited fifteen years for him and he never came along, and Erich Fromm made me understand I wasn't being realistic.

"Everyone I get close to now I'm closer to than the person before because I'm getting better at the art of loving."

FBI Chief J. Edgar Hoover, plus Karl Marx's best known book, made him become a Communist.

Peter Patrick Mendelssohn, seventy-three years old, merchant-marine sailor, longshoreman, union organizer, now a people's advocate in San Francisco, said it happened back in the 1930s.

"Hoover was in Detroit, and he pulled one of the dirtiest, rottenest things I ever saw done.

"A bunch of people were speaking in the county square where you were allowed to speak. They turned out to be Communists although at that time I didn't even know what a Communist was.

"Hoover's men went in with baseball bats and just beat the living hell out of every one of them. A lot of those guys were injured for the rest of their lives. Then they put them in jail.

"They grabbed a bunch that weren't Communists—people in the audience who just wanted to see what was going on. They grabbed everybody they could and put them on buses, took them to Canada, stuck them on a boat going to Russia, and dumped them there.

"And that got me mad, see? That's why I read *Das Kapital* by Karl Marx and turned Communist. I was a Communist for a good many years, and I spread it wherever I sailed all over the world."

Mendelssohn stopped being a Communist "when I visited Russia and couldn't find any Communists among the little people." The experience helped him "appreciate those little people more," he says.

A book showed Paresia Jackson a better way to discipline her children.

"I don't whip my kids the way my mother used to beat us, and us not even knowing what we were getting a whipping for."

Mrs. Jackson is at work before six every morning as a laundry maid at the Laurel Motor Inn in San Francisco. *Baby and Child Care* by Dr. Benjamin Spock, a study of child care up to age twelve, made the most difference for her.

"I was one of thirteen kids, and my mother just hollered at us all day long. Now with my own, I learned from that book to talk to them and sit down and tell them what I liked and what I didn't like about what they did instead of jumping up and just beating them first. That happened to us when we were young, and I just raised my kids different from that."

This book made her move halfway across the country to realize a childhood dream.

As a youngster, Ann O'Neill Garcia was "absolutely smitten by my number one hobby and love, horses."

So it was only natural she should find *My Friend Flicka*, a book by Mary Sture-Vasa (pen name Mary O'Hara) about a Wyoming ranch boy and the horse he loved, Flicka.

"I read that book fifty, sixty, maybe more times. I'd finish it and feel lonely, and right away go back and start reading it all over again. I wanted to be with that McLaughlin family, especially with Ken and his horse, and I didn't want to be apart from them for long."

When she was nine, she had her own horse—named Flicka, of course. When she was ten, the book made her decide that someday she would move from southern Illinois to Wyoming. When she was eleven, she wrote the registrar at the University of Wyoming to ask whether she could enroll. Finally at age nineteen, she was able to board a train for her junior year at the university.

"As we began to climb the mountains near Laramie," she recalled, "I found that Mary O'Hara had described everything so well I almost expected to see Ken McLaughlin sitting astride Flicka on the bluffs."

She was so impressed she wrote the author to tell her how accurate the book had been. There never was an answer.

Ann remained in love with Wyoming. She earned her degree, married, had a son and daughter, taught high school English. Summers, she wrote. One of her books for children, about a cave girl and her grandmother, has been accepted by a publisher.

She still remembers the O'Hara words in *My Friend Flicka* that drew her west.

"The distance, the far, empty distance—the wide loneliness. Miles and miles before you come to another house. Just animals. Grass and animals and sky. You can smell the loneliness. No—it's the emptiness you can smell.

"This is almost a desert. And it has this sweet, fresh singing wildness—you can breathe it in, the very moment you wake in the morning. And it lifts you. You could just float out the window into the blue of the sky, young and new like the country."

It's an exciting place but "not a country for sissies," she says today.

"The winter winds rage at a hefty eighty miles an hour, but even then I'm not sorry I listened to Mary O'Hara's call. The prairies, the mountains, the trout streams, the clouds, the low population, and the exciting changeable weather are reasons enough to love this state."

Tony Randall, the versatile and veteran actor, at his home in New York City, told us:

"When I was about fifteen, I discovered Thomas Wolfe. I guess everyone in my generation did, and I went around like a maniac until I was nineteen, I guess, or twenty.

"I think I memorized *Look Homeward, Angel*, that wonderfully written novel of family life in a southern town. I would stop total strangers and read it to them on the street. I was obsessed with it. It was all I thought about for several years. I thought I'd discovered writing.

"At one time, I think I could have recited most of the book—'a stone, a leaf, an unfound door, a stone, a leaf, a door, and all the forgotten faces, which of us, to make it alone, we came into exile, a dark womb'—I just memorized it.

"When I first read it, I knew very well I wanted to be an actor. There was not the slightest doubt in my mind, I had set my course.

"By the time I grew out of it, I *was* an actor."

R. T. Kingman didn't know the title of the book nor the author. But he did remember the difference it made.

Today he's director of the Office of Issues Management for

General Motors Corporation in Washington, D.C., which means he's about as far up the ladder of corporate lobbyists as one can get in this country. But back in 1938...

"I was fourteen years old, living in a totally segregated community, Kansas City, Kansas, and I had a job in a library putting books away in the stacks.

"A little black boy about my own age walked in to the librarian and said:

" 'Can little colored boys use this library?'

"She said they could, and he checked out a book and he left. I can't tell you the title because I never saw it, nor the author either.

"But that had to be the book that made the greatest difference in my life because it was the first time I ever really understood segregation and the problems of growing up black.

"Here's a little boy who doesn't want to marry my sister; all he wants to do is to read a book from the public library, and he has to ask if he has that right.

"That separated me from the opinions of my parents and completely changed my attitude."

––––––––––

When Jimmy Carter was campaigning for the Presidency, reporters often followed him to services at the First Baptist Church in Plains, Georgia. There they heard the Rev. Bruce Edwards preach.

After the 1976 election, Mr. Edwards continued in the news. A black man applied for membership in the all-white church. Mr. Edwards wanted to admit him. Church leaders did not. They fired Mr. Edwards.

Today he is pastor of the Makakilo Baptist Church in Hawaii, twenty miles from Honolulu. His congregation is a cosmopolitan, multi-color, multi-ethnic group that includes blacks and Hawaiians and Filipinos and Chinese and Japanese and Korean and German and Italian and Russian, and—as he puts it—even some whites.

The book that made the greatest difference in Bruce Edwards' life clearly is related to his racial attitudes. It's *The Book of Acts* by Frank Stagg, a commentary on the Book of Acts of the Apostles in the Bible.

He read this for the first time in the early 1970s when he was still in seminary.

"It convinced me that the biblical message in the New Testament is that people should live together, that the barriers that society erects to separate people, the barrier of racism, should be torn down.

"I already was convinced that segregation was wrong from a legal, constitutional point of view. This gave me the added view that it was wrong from a moral point of view, that Christians should attempt to tear these barriers down."

Mr. Edwards went to the Plains church on January 1, 1975. It was his first pastorate after being graduated from the seminary. He was thirty-three years old.

"The first month I was there, I taught a biblical study on the Book of Acts, using Dr. Stagg's theory heavily. There was no problem then.

"There wasn't any problem until there was a real action, until people had to start putting their words into action.

"Christians," he concluded, "have an obligation to tear these barriers down. It seems the last stronghold of racial prejudice is the church. The church seems to have to be dragged by its heels into the mainstream of Christian thought. Ours here is the exception."

Becky Manley, campus staff worker for Intervarsity Christian Fellowship at Reed College, Portland, Oregon, was about to leave for a new assignment as national consultant and had just one more conference to arrange.

She had just read and very much liked *Memo 1976: Some Political Options*, a book about the political choices available to Christians, by a veteran United Press International correspondent who by then was covering the President in the White House. She decided to invite Wesley Pippert to be her major speaker.

So how did that book make the greatest difference in her life?

"I met the author."

And?

"Now I'm Mrs. Pippert." (Becky Pippert's latest book, *Out of the Salt Shaker*, outsold her husband's. It went over 100,000 copies, was selected as the Outstanding Book of 1980 in Spiritual Growth, and is an all-time best-seller for Intervarsity Press. The Pipperts live in Rockville, Maryland. He now covers the U.S. Senate for UPI.)

SEEING YOURSELF IN PRINT

"I read it when I was fourteen, when I didn't feel like anybody understood how I felt. And here is this book about a fourteen-year-old girl who had the same feelings I did. It made me realize I wasn't alone."

In naming a book in which she saw herself mirrored, Nina Keenan, a business writer in Brooklyn, New York, had much in common with many of the people we interviewed.

Their difference was that they felt reassured through books that they were not unique. There was comfort for them in discovering they had company. Others found solutions for problems in the way their literary heroes manage their lives. And some readers changed their life-style or philosophy after reading about a character with whom they identified. Additional readers discovered in their books a dream or a goal or new possibilities worth adopting because they struck a familiar chord.

Several of these discoveries were true for Nina Keenan, who saw herself in *The Heart Is a Lonely Hunter* by Carson McCullers, a story of a little girl struggling to grow up in a southern town.

"It also made me understand I could be a writer. I didn't have to wait to be a mature human being before my feelings could matter to the world. After all, Carson McCullers was pretty young when she wrote that book.

"Most of my friends were having the same feelings I was, and we all were trying very hard to conceal them. The conflict of adolescence is that when you stop getting the approval of the adult world, it takes a whole lot to get enough self-image so you can go along your own path and not care too much about what everybody else is thinking.

"Most teenagers at some point or other decide either to leave their idealism behind and join the mainstream of human society, or they decide to stick to it. So you end up with idealists, or you end up with realists.

"It made me stick with idealism.

"I get picked on. I'm known as the company radical. But I'm not a radical; I'm an idealist. I think there's something to be gained by believing that people are supposed to be good, and will be good if you believe they are, and will make the right choices and do the right things. I get disappointed a lot but at the same time, the only reason ideals are ideals and not reality is that not enough people believe in them.

"I'm still one of the lonely hunters. And that's OK."

———

The Diary of a Young Girl by Anne Frank, the Jewish girl who hid for two years from the Nazis in Holland and died in a concentration camp, made the difference for Bea MacDonald, deputy director, branch libraries of the New York Public Library:

"She and I would have been the same age. It's kept me thinking through the decades, of our different worlds and what happened to each of us. It's made me think of where I was and where she wasn't."

Ben Moon worked for the railroad in Seattle, and his personal life had been unsettled. His book was *Passages* by Gail Sheehy which focuses on crises common to many adults.

"Before, I always thought I was just some kind of weirdo. With the book, it was nice to know everybody else was going through the same thing too."

We were on the Cherokee Indian Reservation in far western North Carolina, and finally we were able to meet a 100 percent Native American.

Laura Hill King was a teacher of Cherokee History and director of the bilingual program in the Cherokee high school near the Goose Creek recreation area. She also was far along the trail toward the Ph.D. at the University of Tennessee. It hadn't been easy.

Her book was *The Velveteen Rabbit* by Margery Williams, a children's story about a stuffed toy and its dreams of becoming a real rabbit.

"The rabbit finds out in the book what it means to become real—real in the sense that you have to go through so many trials and so much pain and grief in order to find yourself.

"Before I read that book, I was caught up in the rat race of trying to achieve, always achieve, achieve. Now I'm finding out that I am very sensitive, and I'm seeing that without the hurt and pain I've been through, I never would have gotten to where I am. It brought back a lot of memories that were very painful, and yet I discovered one can still learn from the pain and become a better person."

My Name Is Asher Lev by Chaim Potok, is an account of the rise of a painter who always does what he is told, and the conflict between his art and his heritage. For Professor Gerald Ottley, director (only the thirteenth since 1847) of the far-famed three-hundred-voice Mormon Tabernacle Choir in Salt Lake City, Utah:

"His life paralleled mine, and so did the way we had to come to grips with our traditional value systems. I learned that every person has to search out his values. From it I knew what direction I was going, and why, when I moved from my campus teaching to the Choir."

Of Time and the River by Thomas Wolfe, is a sequel to *Look Homeward, Angel* that takes Eugene Gant from his Southern hometown through his years at Harvard and beyond. For John Frantz, city librarian of San Francisco:

"It struck an emotional chord. My hormones were visibly active at the time, as were Thomas Wolfe's when he wrote that amazing book, and it made me more aware of my humanity, my own emotional response and psychic needs, and gave me a sense of recognition of myself that I hadn't had until then."

The Tall Woman by Wilma Dykeman, the story of a North Carolina woman from her Civil War marriage to her death thirty years later, was the book for Dolores West, secretary in the Bureau of Indian Affairs, Western Cherokee reservation, North Carolina:

"The woman she wrote about was a mountain woman. I'm a mountain woman, too, and I remember how she overcame obstacles and knew I could, too."

Lee Ambrose, president of a real estate management and development business in Denver, Colorado, named *Henderson the Rain King* by Saul Bellow, the saga of a Connecticut millionaire's efforts to know his inner spirit.

"It typifies people in mid-life situations wondering what there is, and wanting something, and not knowing what it is. At my age, forty-three, I relate to Henderson's searching for something that is terribly undefined. And I feel some of that, realizing that life is finite. There still is a desire to capture something out there, whatever it might be."

He's very modest about it, but he does have a million dollars—and he's still searching. It's something far more valuable than money he seeks.

A book can lead a person to explore a new life.

In the personnel office of Boeing Aircraft in Seattle, Ken Ragland was bored. He'd been at a desk job sixteen years. No longer was it fun to go to work in the morning.

For exercise, he read a half dozen books a week. So he was out of shape, too, flabby and at 210, at least 25 pounds too heavy.

Then one of those books changed his life. It changed the clothes he wore, the work he did, the pay he earned. It caused him to lose

15

weight and also proved he had as much on the ball physically as college students half his age. Most important, it confirmed that his original choice of a life's occupation had been right all along and sent him back to his desk with new vigor and enthusiasm.

The remarkable book that did all this was *Blue Collar Journal*, the first-person story of how a college president learned more about the world of work outside his own.

The author, John Coleman, had been in the campus world most of his life. Without telling anyone at the college, even his trustees, he went to a different city and looked for hard physical-labor jobs.

He dug ditches, made salads, collected garbage. Months later, he went back to the college presidency "able to see my own work and life in a new light."

Much the same thing happened to Ken Ragland. At the age of forty-one, he quit his personnel job and was hired on as a casual laborer for the Seattle post office.

"The kids were grown and away from home, and it was the first time in my life that I was in a position to do exactly what I wanted to do," he remembers. "I wanted to see if I could compete physically as well as intellectually."

His job was loading mail onto boxcars.

"I'll never forget that first night when I got home. I'd been throwing canvas bags weighing anywhere from 40 to 120 pounds. I was exhausted, my arms and legs felt like jelly, but I also was exhilarated. It felt good to be physically drained, and to be able to keep up with the college kids."

In the Christmas mail rush, the job expanded to seven days a week, twelve hours a day. Ragland's muscles hardened and his weight went down to 175. He felt great.

Later he worked one week collecting garbage—"probably just because Coleman had done it; but that was awful and I quit as soon as I could." Then came three months moving heavy parts in the Boeing plant.

By then physical work was boring. He'd learned he needed to work with people, to have intellectual stimulation, so back he went to personnel.

He still thinks it was a good break to find that book—"I never would have recognized what I needed if I hadn't read it."

His advice to other office workers:

"When you reach a point of ennui on your job, when you dread going to work in the morning, when you know your physical condi-

16

tion is deteriorating and you can't really discipline yourself into enough exercise, that's the time to change and see how the other folks live."

His brief return to the physical world has made him "more empathetic with good workers but less sympathetic with the malingerer," Ragland says.

"I'm more impatient now with the person who doesn't put in a full day's work, because I know the job can be done."

———

"Being able to change a tire on our car. Sometimes I had difficulty getting off the lugs, or whatever it is you call them. But I'd be all alone, and if I wanted to get to town or back home, there was no one else to get that tire changed."

And:

"Getting enough groceries ahead, because we would be snowed in for a month or more at a time."

Finally:

"Helping with the sheep—that is until the coyotes destroyed them, sometimes as many as twenty lambs at a time, just killed for the sport. We'd see those lovely lambs just laid out, dead."

These are some of the memories Grace DeReemer has of the beginnings of her marriage to a Wyoming rancher after living "a protected life back in the small town of Marshfield, Wisconsin."

Her book is *The Egg and I* by Betty MacDonald, an account of a city girl's attempt to manage an isolated chicken farm.

"It gave me company; it was so much like my own life. I came from the city, and I was on a ranch for the first time, and all these things confronted me, and sometimes I just did not know how to deal with them."

There were three sons, and Mrs. DeReemer saw to it they had plenty to read. Thirty books at a time she'd take back to them because the round trip from the ranch to the nearest library was eighty miles.

———

Today Ron Arruda is on the makeup staff of *Sky and Telescope*, an astronomy magazine in Cambridge, Mass., but he well remembers the book that made the greatest difference in his life when he read it at age sixteen.

"It was *Our Lady of the Flowers* by Jean Genet, and it opened to me my homosexual self, so long repressed. I learned there was a rich

17

aesthetic to being gay. It validated those feelings of love which before the book I could not admit."

These readers needed to feel they "belonged," and found help in books. Still other persons feel handicapped in different ways, but also find answers on the printed page.

YOU CAN, TOO, DO IT

A handicap can be an injury or a disease, shyness or the inability to read. Whatever the problem, many of our interviewees found books helped.

Sometimes first aid came from a self-help book, sometimes from fictional characters who overcame obstacles. Whatever the means, the books said it was worth trying one more time.

The readers who found their books made this kind of difference spoke of no small problems:

Facing violence in a tough neighborhood.

Shifting careers in mid-life.

Braving racial prejudice alone.

Adjusting after losing a limb.

This last was Russ Wentworth's situation. Today he is a successful educational administrator, dean of continuing education and dean of the university college at Wichita State University.

But in 1944, at age nineteen, he was in a hospital in England, sent back from France minus his left arm, shot off soon after D-Day. Sad and discouraged, he hadn't even looked at the title of the book he picked up from the top of a stack brought around by an aide. In his mind, he ran over and over:

Would any girl ever look at him again? Were women interested in men with only one arm?

The book turned out to be *Fair Stood the Wind for France* by Herbert Ernest Bates, popular during World War II. It was about an airman shot down during the war who lost an arm in the crash. A French family hid him from the Germans, the daughter nursed him back to health, and they fell in love.

"It must have been written by an amputee or one who was close to an amputee," Wentworth remembers. "The author really knew all the feelings I was going through.

"It gave me the courage to do battle, to come back, to say to myself, 'You can, too, be a human being again.' "

Soon after he was flown back to the U.S., Russ met Carolyn. Their four children now are all grown.

As a youngster small for his age, he lived in a tough area where neighborhood rowdies regularly threatened to beat him up. But George Gloss found that books could help him whip that problem.

"I went to the East Boston public library and finally was old enough to get a membership card. This entitled me to listen to the story-hour lectures of Mrs. Mary Cronin, a wonderful woman, large and with a florid face. She had a mellifluous flow of language and she would tell about all the greats, about Ulysses and all the rest, of Roman and Greek mythology.

"I then would go upstairs and get those books, illustrated by N. C. Wyeth and Rackham and other great artists, and I would take them home and read them.

"What happened then is that I became the storyteller of the neighborhood, and very simply this kept me from getting beaten up. They all knew me, and nobody would touch the storyteller. I'd have about a dozen of my own age, I'd tell 'em the stories and maybe embellish them just a little, too."

Today, George Gloss owns the Brattle Book Shop in Boston, the "oldest antiquarian book shop in the United States." Started in 1825, the shop stocks used books by the hundreds of thousands.

It also is subject to fires, and Gloss has had to rebuild it three times, the latest after an early-1980 $1 million blaze consumed 450,000 volumes. But the books that were lost in the fire—the page from the Gutenberg Bible, the Gold Rush diary, the first editions—weren't the ones that made the greatest difference to him. What really stuck in his memory were the books used for the children's story hours, and the "you can, too, do it" message that they planted.

The Hobbit by Tolkien, a tale of an imaginary creature's adventures in a land of dwarfs, elves, goblins, dragons and humans, is her book. She chose The Hobbit, "because it showed me you can overcome your handicaps and be whatever you want to be."

And Kathy Coster did have some handicaps.

"I was nine years old before I could tell left from right, and then only because I had my sister mark my arms, and my left arm was the one with the white spot. Sometimes even today I have to look down at my arm and remember that to tell which way to turn when I'm driving.

19

She had trouble right from the start of school.

"My first grade teacher told my mother to hit me with a ruler because I was lazy. The problem, I know, was not that I was lazy. It was a real disability.

"I was promoted through seven grades even though I couldn't read. Someone in the Walla Walla school system, my mother never would tell me who, advised her it was a waste of time for me to go on to high school."

Finally, she was placed in special education classes. And that worked.

Kathy was almost twenty when she finished high school. Then she flunked the training program to become a licensed practical nurse.

"But I went back and took the vocabulary courses they wanted me to take, passed the course, worked four years, and got the associate degree from junior college."

When we had our interview, Kathy was thirty years old. She also was a senior in Seattle University. How well she had applied the lesson from *The Hobbit* was reflected in her grades of the quarter before. She had taken a full load, fifteen credits, including a tough course in statistics.

And she had made the honor roll.

———

Betty Osborne, a nurse in Peoria, Ill., knew what could happen, so when she went in for a biopsy on her breast, she also just "happened" to take along Norman Cousins' book, *Anatomy of an Illness*.

It was well she did, too, because the examination led to a mastectomy and a year of chemotherapy.

"During those early days of terror and despair that no one could help me with, Norman Cousins' record of his own confrontation with possible death and his climb back to health through hope and self-healing literally sustained and comforted me. It gave me the hope to rebuild my life and my health. And now I feel great!"

———

Dr. Sol Gordon is an internationally known author, public speaker, educator. One of the country's experts on adolescent sexuality, he is professor of child and family studies and director of the Institute for Family Research and Education at Syracuse University.

His book is only forty-one pages written by Martin Buber, *The Way of Man*. One of its messages, he said, is that "we don't have to compare ourselves with anybody else, for God has created each of us in a unique way.

"The difference that made for me was that I did have a tendency to downgrade myself a little and think of all the people who were luckier, happier, or more famous than I. It helped put my life into perspective. Once having recognized that I don't have to compare myself with anyone else, I am free, with a lot of energy for all the things I really want to do."

To the Lighthouse by Virginia Woolf—a description of the thoughts and feelings of a party of people gathered in successive summers at a house on the Scottish coast—was the book for Mrs. Margaret Wainwright, Seattle housewife and mother of five. Of the author, she said:

"She had such handicaps. She had such physical problems. She had such sorrow. She was odd. She was peculiar. Because I could identify with her and sympathize with her, it made things easier. It makes your own problems not so enormous if you can look back on somebody who's produced despite so many drawbacks in her life."

How to Win Friends and Influence People by Dale Carnegie, a guide for pleasing people through recognizing their need for personal importance: this was the book for Tex Potter, Cottage Grove, Oregon, logger and past president of the International Woodworkers of America, a union of 3,500 loggers working for six different companies.

"I told myself one day when I was forty-two years old, 'Old fellow, you've logged your own timber, you like loggers, you like their outlook on life, just why do you stay in the grocery business?' The company thought I was crazy, but my only regret was that I didn't start earlier. It was the happiest time of my life.

"What the book did was channel me into that path, logging. It grew me; it taught me to look at people, to value them, to accept them. It gave me confidence I hadn't had. You see, I only went through the seventh grade."

How-to-do-it books made a practical difference for Jean Wilson, after thirty-seven years the senior waitress at the famous Durgin-Park restaurant near the fishing wharves in the Boston harbor.

"I remodeled my whole house, the plumbing, electrical, pipes, painting, carpentry, papering, window glass, and roofing. That wasn't so much in vogue when I did it, back in the 1940s and '50s, but I just got inspired."

Madame Curie: A Biography by her daughter, Eve Curie, tells of her mother's discovery and lifelong study of radium and radioactivity. For Shirley Littler, Cheyenne, treasurer of the state of Wyoming:

"It gave me a vision of the world. It helped me decide I could do whatever I'd set out to do."

You might remember the picture in the papers.

It was 1961. New Orleans had just started desegregating its public schools. At William Frantz Elementary, all the white parents had withdrawn their children. Just one pupil remained. Tiny—and black—Ruby Bridges sat there, all alone in her classroom, the only student left. And there she sat all year.

The book in her life?

" 'Tar-Baby', the story of a rabbit. When people struck out at Tar-Baby, they got stuck to him. Because of their striking out, they were the ones who got hurt. But it had a happy ending, Tar-Baby got out of it OK."

She learned to read during that first grade, and read this Joel Chandler Harris story then.

"Now as I look back on it, maybe the story of Tar-Baby is what gave me the courage to go on, because it was a lonesome year, a very lonesome one, and I didn't understand why it had to be like that. It took some doing to stay in there all year long. But I did, and that sort of had a happier ending than I was expecting, too."

He teaches cooking, Creole cooking, and he knows the best places in town for crawfish bisque or etoufee, places where you get real home cookin' not generally known to tourists.

The other things Leon Soniat does in New Orleans are write a cooking column for the *Times-Picayune* and make syndicated television shorts about cooking.

Such activity may seem a considerable leap from the book that made the greatest difference in his life. When he was twelve, he ran across Will Durant's *The Story of Philosophy*, the basic thoughts of the great philosophers from Plato to John Dewey.

"I had heard the word *philosophy* but I didn't know what it was. Since then I must have read that book forty times. It made me realize that life is not just something you endure from the time you are born until the time you die. There are so many things you can think about. I became aware of ontology and cosmology and psychology and logic and epistemology and things like that.

"The more I read it, the more I figured that what man can conceive, man can achieve. It's almost impossible to limit man's achievements. His potentialities are virtually unlimited."

For a special meal, he recommends Chez Helen, Dooky-Chase, or K-Paul's. The last was very good when we ate there. We shared a table with a newspaper restaurant critic. All gave it a grade of Mmmm!

Island of the Blue Dolphins is by Scott O'Dell, the story of an Indian girl left behind when tragedy decimates her tribe and of how she manages not only to exist but to find joy and comfort in her isolation. For Evelyn Philon, computer programming student, Tampa College in Florida:

"It made me realize that even when you are all alone, you still can make it."

There were bombings. One killed a University of Wisconsin graduate student—and sent Gloria Gehrman to Moscow.

She was working in Milwaukee, and "since people kept referring to anarchism, I wanted to know more about it. So I read about Emma Goldman, for many years a leader of anarchists in America and Europe. I was the first in thirty-five years to check out *Living My Life*, her autobiography.

"It was at a time I was trying to make a break from the community I was brought up in, and I just decided to leave. I just decided that if this lady could go and do all those things, then I guess I could go and run away from home."

Miss Gehrman now is the director of the Moscow public library. Moscow, Idaho, that is.

Self-Renewal by John Gardner is the book in which the former president of the Carnegie Foundation and the founder of Common Cause examines how a good society can protect all its members without crushing the individual. For Arthur Smith, Logan, Utah psychologist:

"It's given me hope when I've been down. It's given me more of a purpose in life, helped me remember that the purpose is to matter, to make a difference."

When Silva Barsumyan took over the job of director of the public library in Union City, N.J., she was all of twenty-five years old. But she'd already had a dozen years of library experience and

23

had a feeling that there was some kind of solution for every difficulty.

"I got that from reading *The Mill on the Floss* by Eliot," she reported. "In the book, there is a minor character with a club foot who rises above his handicap. I sort of understood that because I've had a health problem that used to keep me from attending school.

"I figured anyone who could write a book like that was a very important person who was to be believed. If she could make that character beat his trouble, then I could overcome mine. And that's been my theme ever since."

The surgeon bent over, outlining in purple the lump under the eye.

"Let me make three points," he said. "Ninety-nine percent of these are malignant. But 99 percent have not spread. And 99 percent do not recur."

The patient was soothed.

"By the way," the surgeon continued, "why don't you ask that question of yours, and see who can answer it?"

Medical students were standing around observing. The patient had a towel over his eyes, so he had to ask anyone in general:

"What book made the greatest difference in your life?"

A pause. Silence. Then:

"*The Power of Positive Thinking* by Norman Vincent Peale."

"Who said that?"

"I'm John Zangermeister."

"Where are you from?"

"Bellevue, Ohio."

"What year are you?"

"This is my first year in medical school. I did my undergraduate work at Case Western Reserve."

"What difference did that book make?"

"I read it when I was fifteen, when I was really searching to find myself, when my self-esteem was low and my anxiety about the future high, and I really needed a boost and some self-assurance. It gave me a lot more self-confidence."

"And doctors need a lot of self-confidence, right?"

At that point, the surgeon cut in.

"We'll send this to the lab, so you just lie quiet now until the report comes back."

I did lie quietly.

24

The report did come back.

And the surgeon was right on all three counts.

It's obvious that for a book to make a difference, people have to know how to read, an ability most of us take for granted. But some adults never can read, sometimes because they were slow learners or had poor teachers, and sometimes because they never were permitted to attend school.

This last was the case for Betty Elliott.

THE FIRST BOOK SHE EVER READ—
AT AGE THIRTY

Catherine Gillie, Columbus, Ohio, wife of a judge, mother of four, part-time nurse, heard a radio commercial.

"It said seventy-seven thousand persons in central Ohio did not know how to read. I didn't believe there was anyone like that."

She and the judge took the four Saturday morning training sessions offered by the Columbus Literacy Council.

Mrs. Gillie: "Then I was assigned a student, and I called her. Her voice was so soft I could hardly hear her. It was obvious that I had awakened her, but when I said, 'I've been assigned to be your tutor,' a shriek of joy came over that telephone.

"She was so delighted. Several times before she had tried to get help. Once she even telephoned the Columbus Board of Education to say she couldn't read, and the secretary there wouldn't believe her. Because of her use of language and the way she presented her ideas so well, the secretary was sure she was a college graduate playing a prank."

The student was Betty Elliott, something over thirty years old (she isn't sure because there are no records), who was orphaned at three weeks and taken to New York City by a woman who wanted her to help around the house. She remembers having to stand on a chair to wash dishes and diapers. Whenever the truant officer came around, the woman would say, "Don't bother with her; she's not right, you know."

Never a day in school and not able to read a word. She recalls:

"I get surprised when I think back to when I had to memorize things and wasn't able to put them down on paper."

What she did was fake it a lot. She "wrote" her name—but

actually she drew the letters. She made reports at the end of her night shift as a cottage mother in Franklin Village, a children's home, by calling a friend and telling her what she wanted to say. Slowly the friend would spell out the letters, and laboriously Betty would print them in capitals.

"I had no idea you could picture letters because I didn't know what reading and writing were all about. Now I can close my eyes and see that *a* and *b* and you know that's marvelous."

Mrs. Gillie would go to the Elliott home for lessons: "We both cried a great deal at the beginning. We spent many sessions with not too much time reading but with her telling about her life. Never before, she said, had any individual been personally interested in her. Many friends, because she's a very friendly person, but never anyone that interested."

Elliott: "People think if you can't read or write, you're stupid."

To cover up, she learned numbers. She counted on her fingers and found how to make change. She couldn't read labels at the grocery, but she knew how to shake the cans. If the contents rattled, they were peas. If the can was heavy, it was fruit. She even could tell pears from peaches without pictures.

Gillie: "It's fascinating, the extent to which people learn to cope and work around the printed word. It takes immeasurable use of energy and brainpower and time and money, but to a small extent, it can be done.

"After two months, I asked her whether she was able to see any difference at work or anywhere else because she could begin to read. Betty answered:

" 'I notice now that when I look in the mirror, I'm smiling.' "

Over about three years, there were some eighty tutoring sessions, ninety or so minutes each, sometimes twice a week, sometimes only once a month when both were very busy.

Elliott: "Another surprise, when you see on paper the word that you have been holding up here in your mind and rattling it around, then you see it there and begin to make some sense out of it. It's surprise; it's happiness.

"The first day I was able to do one word, one word as I have in my book, to know that I could spell it out; it stood out so much for me, just to know I could spell it and hear it. That was so neat, the way the sounds came together. I can see it; I can hear the letters."

(The word was *s-p-y.*)

Gillie: "She's such an intelligent person, with such compassion, such wisdom. She could write a psychology book about working with children. And she accomplished all this with no models. A very wise, very smart person."

Elliott: "If I could just tell it all, if people only knew exactly how I felt then and also bring it up to now, it would be some story. It would be like—like it's not the truth. I have all intentions some day to write that for others to know."

Gillie: "I've been involved in all the things you do as your children are growing up, and I've thought they were good causes, and you put your shoulder to the wheel, and that's fine.

"But this is different, seeing a whole world open up to one person who had been seeing the world through a long tube without much light at the end. That's the most exciting thing that can happen."

Betty Elliott's book: the one from which she read her very first word, *The New Streamlined English Series: In the Valley*.

Happy ending: She won a prize for reading the most books of any student in the literacy program her first year.

BOOKS THAT INSPIRED CAREERS

A book considered "very dirty" at the time—*A Farewell to Arms* by Ernest Hemingway— got Les Asheim interested in library work.

"When I was in high school, the board banned that book in the public library in Seattle. But the librarian, seeing I was a serious reader, pointed out to me that although she was not permitted to buy the book, I could read it in installments in *Scribner's* magazine, which the library had right there on the shelf.

"That began to open up the library field to me, that and the fact that libraries protect your right to read rather than censor."

Hemingway's novel about a young American disillusioned with World War I influenced a career that for Asheim included being dean of the University of Chicago's Graduate Library School and member of the American Library Association staff. Now he holds a distinguished chair on the faculty of the library school at the University of North Carolina, Chapel Hill.

His experience was typical of many who found a book that inspired their life's work. In the following stories, readers from ages sixteen to seventy-five discovered their careers from books—but age didn't seem to make as much difference as stage. You have to be ready for the suggestion. Once you are, what someone writes can make a significant impression.

27

Clare Boothe Luce, playwright, editor, author, Congresswoman, ambassador, director of fifteen organizations, holder of eleven honorary degrees, winner of eighteen medals and awards:

"What made the greatest differences were the plays—and I will not pick out just one—the plays of Bernard Shaw, which resolved me at about the age of fifteen or sixteen that if I could make it, I'd become a playwright. That made the difference of pointing the way I wanted to go and that *was* the way I went.

"And I had the great pleasure of telling George Bernard Shaw, when my play *The Women* opened in London—that's the first time I met him—I was able to say 'Had I not read your plays, I would not be here in London today,' and that was true enough."

From her home in Honolulu, Mrs. Luce added:

"The truth of the matter is that everything makes a difference, and many things, as you read, change your mind.

"There even was a point in my life when I was in my late twenties that I became for the space of a year a concerned Marxist, as a result of reading *Das Kapital*. And then became unconcerned when I learned really what the Lincoln Brigade was all about.

"So one reads and then what one reads is either confirmed by experience or is denied by experience, and all else, I think, falls in the realm of faith."

———

In Wilmington, North Carolina in high school, Herman Postma read *Our Plundered Planet* by Fairfield Osborn.

"It warned people about the earth's limited resources and how we were wasting them. It was one of the first to say this, well before the modern environmentalists. But even more important, it was perhaps the earliest book that clearly stated not only the limitation of resources but also ways to solve the problem.

"It indicated that through technology, there were ways to alter the gloomy forecast, and that's why I became interested in technological solutions to problems, which is exactly what my whole professional career has been about."

That career? Dr. Postma heads the three thousand professionals who staff the National Laboratory at Oak Ridge, Tennessee, the lab that started with the atomic energy development and that now conducts research on energy and environmental issues.

———

Battle Cry by Leon Uris, is about the Marines in World War II. For Officer James Fox, first generation Irish-American, New York

City Police Department, stationed at the corner of Fifth Avenue and Forty-second Street:

"It made me volunteer for the U.S. Marine Corps when I was graduated from high school. The book really was right about the *esprit de corps* the corps has."

In high school, he spent a lot of time in sports and not much with studies. Then he found the book that turned him around—*One Hundred Great Lives* edited by John Allen.

"These were short biographies, five or six or seven pages each, of scientists, inventors, social reformers, writers, that sort of person. I really liked them, and that led to a lot more reading. My grades went up, then my college grades were considerably better than the high school ones, and eventually they got up enough so I was admitted to medical school, and that made a heck of a difference in my life."

Now it's Erwin Busiek, M.D., of Springfield, Missouri.

Sometimes, the subject is revelation.

In New York City, the general manager of the Newspaper Advertising Bureau is a researcher, author, fellow of the American Psychological Association, former president of both the American and the World Associations of Public Opinion Research.

Leo Bogart was seventeen and just in college when he read Lewis Mumford's *The Culture of Cities*, a survey of the history of cities with proposals for improving them.

"As a humanistic statement of the possibilities of the social sciences, it was a revelation to me as a teenager just beginning to explore the meaning of the world.

"The erudition, the vision, the combination of ideas and reference materials from the vast, different resources, the lucid quality of the writing, the sense of passion that imbued it, the notion of what social life was all about—eventually I became a social scientist and it shaped my career."

The Diffusion of Innovations by Everett Rogers, which is about how new ideas and practices become known and adopted. For Kerry Byrnes, sociologist with the International Fertilizer Development Center, Muscle Shoals, Alabama:

"That was the text in a sophomore course in college. Until then, I'd just been shopping around, but this book lighted my interest in a career. Ten years later, I wrote my dissertation on the same subject and since then, it's been my professional career."

Candide by Voltaire, the adventures of a young man as he wanders about the world, an inquiry into the nature of good and evil. For Professor Willard Thompson, head of the advertising program and also director of the summer session at the University of Minnesota:

"It made me suddenly realize there was something more than sports magazines to read. It suddenly made me want to read things that were important. I'd been pretty happy-go-lucky and I didn't have much in the way of grades, but after that, my senior year marks improved considerably and I was able to go on to graduate school and eventually to teach."

If he had become a doctor, as his physician father wanted him to do, "I'd have been following in my father's footsteps and not have had the right size shoes," said Mike Bessie, senior vice-president of Harper & Row, New York book publishers.

Instead, Vincent Sheean's *Personal History* appeared at just the right time. This account of Sheean's life covers him from age eighteen at the University of Chicago to years of newspaper work here and abroad.

"I was just on the verge of deciding what to do with my life, and that book confirmed my conviction that the right thing to do was to become a journalist rather than a doctor, and a foreign correspondent as a journalist."

Bessie was a war correspondent for *Look* magazine at the start of World War II before he started publishing books.

The New Science of Politics by Eric Voegelin, about political science as understood before 1900, was the book for William Havard. He is an editor, author, chairman of political science at Vanderbilt University, former Dean of Arts and Sciences, Virginia Tech, and former president of the New England, Northeastern and Southern Political Science Associations:

"That book pretty much determined what sort of political scientist I'd be. I would have gone to law school if I hadn't encountered it and the author."

For Daniel Boorstin, author and The Librarian of Congress, it was Edward Gibbon's *Decline and Fall of the Roman Empire*, which radiates the author's enchantment with the grandeur of Rome.

"It awakened me to what the writing of history could be.

"Gibbon was an amateur, and I think that is the greatest vocation of all, for an amateur is a lover, and a lover is a person who does something not because he gets paid for it but because he can't help it and he must do it.

"Gibbon was not a dogmatist. His humanity was broad and he saw experience as something that was iridescent, which had a different meaning depending on where you stood or where you sat. In that way, he opened the world in ways a dogmatic historian never could.

"In my study at home, where I still do my writing and try to be a historian myself, I have an engraving of Edward Gibbon, who looks down at me with his triple chin and encourages me to do some of the things he did."

Karl Menninger's *The Human Mind* was both a beginning and a turning point in his life, Dr. William O'Brien of Novato, California, testifies.

"It was 1944 during the war, and I'd gotten busted and was doing time in the guardhouse. Books were considered contraband, but I found one in the trash and out of cussedness or defiance, smuggled it into the stockade.

The Human Mind records "an enlightened treatment of mental illness and criminal behavior," and it's not simple reading.

"I'd been graduated from the high school in Berkeley, California, but I read at no better than the second or third grade. I was functionally nonliterate, so with this book, I taught myself to read. And then it was a turning point, too, because my subsequent professional life has been devoted to research and treatment of delinquent youth."

The California tax revolt dried up the funding for Dr. O'Brien's youth counseling work. Today he is a tugboat skipper.

Cecily Foxley had taken her first two degrees in English, and was right on schedule in preparing to become an English professor.

Then she was widowed and went through a period of depression.

"Finally, though, I decided I did want to live and not only that, I wanted to make a difference in people's lives."

So she changed her academic major to counseling, earned the

doctorate, married again, and became Professor Cecily Foxley Smith, assistant vice-president for student services at Utah State University.

Her books-that-made-the-difference were written by William Shakespeare, the great seventeenth century English poet and dramatist.

"He touched on all types of emotions and all types of characters, and while I had studied his books for years when I was majoring in English, I found they also helped me in understanding human behavior. In fact, they helped as much as any book on psychology I ever read."

———

John Forsyth *thought* he was going to be an engineer. He *knew* he wasn't going to teach. Then he read a computer language manual, and it turned his life quite around.

"It had this fascinating way of representing descriptions of solutions to problems," and he liked that. He tried it, and also liked teaching. Now he teaches computer operations at Michigan State University.

"What I didn't realize for a long time, though, was what I was really supposed to be learning was a different kind of human communication process. I thought you were supposed to make the machine work, but that's not the most important thing. What's most important is that through the computer, a properly educated human being can with great sophistication communicate with another properly educated human being."

———

Sometimes the way to a new career doesn't present itself until you're well into the adult years.

That's what Joe Howland found when he read Eric Hoffer's *The True Believer*, about how persons of great conviction can promote minority ideas until they lead to significant change.

"Hoffer's book gave me the urge to take the underdog side of a question and really see what they're complaining about and what could be done about it. That's what got me interested in management."

Before the book, he'd been "just a writer." After it, he rose quickly to become assistant to the president of Scott Grass Seed Company, then a top executive with another firm. Now he's a professor of horticulture at the University of Nevada at Reno, and specializes in marketing strategy.

———

The difference, the man said, was that he jumped from a staff job with the Associated Press into national syndication almost overnight. The difference was the "Terry and the Pirates" comic strip, a leading escapist vehicle of its day (which was during the depression of the 1930s when escapism was both needed and welcome).

Milton Caniff was twenty-seven. His editor was Captain Joseph Patterson, publisher of the *New York News*, the top boss himself. One day Patterson called in the artist.

"Here," he said, "read these two books. They'll fit that comic strip we've been talking about."

From *Wuthering Heights*, by Emily Brontë, a gothic romance set on the Yorkshire moors, Caniff "got the unrequited love story of Heathcliffe and Kathy, a thesis I've used ever since."

And from *Pirates of the China Coast*, author long since forgotten, Caniff picked out Lai Choi Sam, meaning "mountain of wealth," who was the leading woman pirate along the China Coast.

"That's who became the Dragon Lady."

At its height, "Terry and the Pirates" was sold by the Chicago Tribune-New York News Syndicate to 650 papers with millions of readers. People who couldn't miss the strip when they were youngsters "turn up today as college presidents and all sorts of other good things," Caniff commented.

Moreover, good ideas do not die. "In a very real sense, I still use the same thesis in the 'Steve Canyon' strip; it's really a spin-off of 'Terry and the Pirates.' The difference now is I own 'Steve Canyon,' and I did not own 'Terry and the Pirates.' "

The company that every year produces more titles than all the rest of the publishing world put together was near death at its beginning—in more ways than one.

It all began in the back rooms of an undertaking parlor, with a total start-up capital of only $1,500 plus an Eastman Kodak how-to-do-it book the boss couldn't understand.

In 1936, Eugene Power was thirty-one and director of sales for the Edwards Publishing house in Ann Arbor, Michigan. He had this notion about being able to make very tiny pictures of all the pages of a book. Microfilming, it was called.

"But I had a good many deficiencies," Power recalls. "I bought the best book there was available, Kodak's *Motion Picture Laboratory Practices*, but I still couldn't understand."

One more time through, one final desperate reading—and suddenly, everything became clear. Power negotiated for the use of two back rooms in a funeral home from seven to midnight, after he

33

finished his regular job. His first project was a short-title catalog of books printed in England, Scotland, Wales, and Ireland, 1474-1640.

And University Microfilms, Incorporated grew and grew until Power sold it to Xerox in the mid-1970s—for $8 million.

In Cheyenne, Wyoming, some say that Dave Pauley is every bit as good a Western artist as Charles M. Russell, the American painter and sculptor whose realistic works in oil and bronze portray Indians and cowboys and animals of the plains and mountains.

Pauley doesn't comment on that, but he does say *Pen and Ink Drawings* and other Russell books made the most difference to him.

"I learned my art from them. Them and a course by correspondence."

Pauley was born in Osage, Wyoming, population three hundred. In World War II, he was a navy air transport flier. He's been painting the Old West since about 1968.

What does an artist feel when he's painting?

"In my case, high adventure.

"High adventure is a big thing with me. I think when I put mountains and plains, sagebrush and so forth on canvas and cowboys or Indians or mountain men riding over the hill, it's a high adventure they're looking for—and I see."

When he was thirteen, Thomas Horne, now an attorney in Phoenix, Arizona, read *The Ugly American* by Lederer and Burdick.

"It describes people who do good things and people who louse things up," he remembers. "A lot of people who loused things up in that book had political power—Congressmen and Senators who didn't know what they were doing and just went around messing things up.

"One of the lessons I drew from that is that if you want to do good, you've not only got to want to but you also ought to get into a position where you have some power. That influenced me toward a career that would enable me some day to become involved in politics in a serious way, so I can do some good in an effective way."

Horne hasn't yet run for political office. "But the time will come," he's sure.

Andrew Cook, of Hull, Mass., named a "benchmark book" that taught him skills, eased the tension of daily life, and relieved the pain of arthritis.

It is *Boatbuilding in Your Own Backyard*, by Sam Rabl.

34

"In the author's enthusiastic confidence for his reader, I found confidence in myself," he says. "In the dream-inspiring line drawings of boats, I found relaxation. From the pages of this book, I built my first boat. After developing arthritis at age thirty and knowing I couldn't continue to do heavy craft work, I began to study to become a yacht designer. I'm doing quite well, thanks."

Katherine Hatch, today a foreign correspondent in Cuernavaca, Mexico, received Richard Halliburton's *Complete Book of Marvels* "at the dining room table in Kansas City on my twelfth birthday, and I've never been the same since."

This was another world and whetted her appetite for travel adventure. And yes, she adds, "I've splashed the water of the Blue Grotto, felt the wind blowing down the snowy slopes of Popocatepetl, marveled at the Panama Canal. I'm still working on that old fabulous list that opened my eyes and my life thirty-four years ago—and I still have the book."

Edison, a biography by Matthew Josephson, a chronicle of the man, his struggle for creation in a world of sound, and his philosophical views. For Harley Stuntz, seventy-five, formerly of Fort Wayne, Indiana, now of Ft. Myers, Florida and a guide in the Thomas A. Edison summer home, this proved a career change can come almost at retirement time:

"In fact, I did retire and came here when I was sixty-two and I didn't have anything to do. That book gave me an incentive to do something besides sit around. I wanted to do something that would help others."

Books also help others to help themselves. For one family in Minnesota, the way to escape civilization's stress and to settle in the wilderness came from a book.

CAN YOU GET AWAY FROM IT ALL?

You go north of Duluth, Minnesota, 152 miles north along the highway that edges Lake Superior. Through Superior National Forest, then Grand Portage State Forest, finally the Grand Chippewa Indian Reservation.

The population of the whole county is only 4,400. The largest town is Grand Portage, population 350, mostly American Indians.

Fifteen miles still farther north is the Pigeon River, which divides the United States from Canada, where the customs house and border station used to stand before they built the bridge to the road in Ontario.

If a person wanted to "get away from it all," where better?

So Professor Nat Hart and his wife Joanne thought in 1969. They had just read *Living the Good Life—How to Live Sanely and Safely in a Troubled World* by Scott and Helen Nearing, and they were inspired. The Nearings wrote about their escape from the city, their creating a place on a farm free from dependence on society.

Joanne explains:

"It had been a pretty hectic decade. We decided to simplify our life. There wasn't any place more beautiful than the far northeastern tip of Minnesota, so we moved here into what had been the customs buildings.

"Nat teaches eighteenth-century English literature at the University of Minnesota branch in Morris, and we lived there through the sixties. After we found our new place, he took a sabbatical and read a lot of books and learned how to fix up the old buildings so we could spend the winter there."

When they moved, five of their eight children still lived at home. After the sabbatical, Nat went back to the campus, eight hours drive away, to resume teaching. The family was together again only in summers and vacation breaks and for an occasional weekend for the theatre in Minneapolis.

They have electricity for the power tools but, beyond that, make no concession to comfort. The nearest neighbor is seven miles away. There is no running water, so no bathing ("We built a sauna and discovered it made a wonderful bath"). No central heating, no television, no telephone, only poor radio reception, no plumbing, no washing machine ("I go to Grand Marais, round trip ninety miles, every eight or ten days to do the washing").

They have a cookhouse, a bunkhouse, the professor's study cabin ("no electricity there, but he does with kerosene lamps"), an outhouse a quarter of a mile down the path.

It's cold in winter. Down to forty degrees below zero Fahrenheit "but usually not more than twenty below. Not too bad. It's dry; it's lots more comfortable than I used to be in New Jersey."

The Nearing book gave them ideas. One was that Nat retire early to spend full time in the country. Another was that they could be self-sufficient. Both proved impossible.

"We realized after we moved up here that of course the Near-ings were working with no family. If you have children, you need a cash income; you just absolutely have to have some cash because there are a lot of things you can't grow and that you can't make yourself."

On the other hand, there was a bonus for Joanne. She picked up again on the writing she had stopped to have the children. Her poetry has been published in midwest journals, she gives poetry readings, and she writes a monthly magazine column. She was a state delegate to the White House Conference on Library and Information Services.

There also have been changes in outlook.

"We have a log cabin school, two rooms, two teachers, maybe thirty students, run along the lines of an Indian school. The Indian cultural values are emphasized, and when my youngest, Joe, went there, they were learning the Indian language.

"They didn't get hung up on a lot of things non-Indians generally get hung up on—time, money, the accumulation of goods, prestige, power. They don't seem to be looking for those things. There's much more a feeling that in the long run, things will take care of themselves, will work out, and there isn't any terrific imperative to get ahead."

Is life what they expected?

"No, it's very different. For one thing, you don't leave the world behind. You are definitely part of your society and part of your times. You can't force yourself from it.

"For another, I never dreamed I'd be so dependent upon an automobile. I have to drive forty-eight miles a day just to and from the school bus, ninety miles round trip to the nearest library, thirty miles round trip to the store. We had 209,000 miles on our old Ford station wagon before it gave up the ghost.

"We realize we can't be self-sufficient; we can't raise all our own food. We have a garden every summer, but the growing season is incredibly short. The last frost has come as late as June 25, and the first, as early as August 15."

One of their tenets of life, she told us, is "we adapt to the environment as much as we can, rather than shaping the environment to suit our whims, wishes, needs, whatever. Probably this is a way we most differ from Helen and Scott Nearing in living our own 'good life.' They gardened organically and lived simply, but they were manipulators of their farm, developers within the value system they so eloquently express.

"We, on the other hand, partly because we cannot be entirely self-sufficient, partly because we have discovered values of the Indians we live among, have a commitment to disturbing the natural world as little as possible, adapting our daily lives to the environmental circumstances, and trying for less, not more, whenever there's a choice. It is not possible to be ascetic hermits, and we don't pretend to be that, but we do keep the rhythms of the natural, biological world very much in the front of our plans and our observations."

Joanne describes some of their life and times in her December, 1980 column for *Women's Times*, "a journal for North Country women." In it, she wrote:

"It's clean here, and quiet, we expect the cold and prepare for it, and we are in touch with the out-of-doors. Because wood fires must be tended, we go outside for armloads of logs, pieces of wood split and stacked a season ago to dry in readiness for this snowy day, this chilly wind. Pull on cap and mittens, lace up boots, breathe in dry, sweet air of northwoods winter, haul the loaded sled down the path to the bunkhouse, straining a little, panting a little, enjoying the action. Then as dusk closes in, after the perils of the school bus run are behind and dinner fills the cookhouse with delicious odors, contemplate with time for homework, study, library books, letter writing, journals.

"Tonight, this cabin is cozy, the barrel stove is sloughing and radiating, the thermometer reads twelve degrees below, and I'm going outside again to check another stove, to plug in the car, to see the stars. Behind me in the reflecting snow, my lighted cabin gleams like a jewel box, but down in the clearing there is only heavenly light, the planets seem astonishingly near, and across the river up in the north, the Fire Dancers begin their awesome flicker.

"Later as I pull the down comforter up around my ears, I'll be conscious of those northern lights. I'll sleep and dream like my city cousins, but when I wake before dawn, I'll be outside again, walking on the snowy path toward the cookhouse to prepare breakfast, listening for the last sound before ice seals over the running river and winter quiet settles on us like a cloak."

Another interesting American sought to get away from it all back in the mid-1800s. He built a cabin by the side of a pond, and his description of those two years of simple life "free from the world" has become a longed-for standard of life for a host of believers.

Roland Robbins remembers July 4, 1945 very clearly. The weather was great, and he loved to play tennis and really wished he could. Instead, out of a sense of duty, he went to the one hundredth anniversary observation of Henry David Thoreau's move to Walden Pond.

Robbins had just completed a booklet about the origin and meaning of the Minuteman statue that stood in Lexington, Massachusetts and that had been a World War II rallying symbol in the United States.

At the celebration, an argument took place about the exact location of the Thoreau cabin. The official in charge suggested that "Robbins is a great researcher. Maybe he could look into it for us."

"Well, of course I was flattered by that," Robbins recalls. "After all, I was a window-washer and house-painter by trade, and a high school dropout, in fact. I got a ninety-five-cent copy of *Walden* and read it, but I soon found there was no use of trying to listen to Thoreau identify where his cabin stood. He didn't write *Walden* when he lived there; *Walden* came out seven years after he left.

"As you read *Walden*, it's just as though you're sitting there looking out the window. His style was so beautiful that way. Actually, that isn't what he saw at all.

"I gave up on *Walden* and went back to Thoreau's original journals, and they proved he had embellished them later in *Walden*.

"There was a journal entry: 'I went down to the pond and brought two cart loads of stones up the hill for my chimney foundation,' and that foundation is what I looked for, and that is what I eventually found."

After Robbins located the footings of the original cabin, his fame as a pick-and-shovel historian grew. One project led to another. There was no time any more for window washing, and he became a full-time consultant on colonial and early American landmarks and their restoration.

He built a reproduction of the Thoreau cabin in his back yard and says, "That cabin wasn't just a lean-to or a hut, either. It was ten by fifteen feet, plastered, brick chimney, brick fireplace, shingled roof, shingled siding, a real minihouse."

Robbins became president of the Thoreau society and still is on its executive board. (He also found time to play on the Lexington tennis team and in 1955, at the age of forty-seven, won the men's singles title in a tough five-setter.)

You are welcome to visit the Robbins version of the Thoreau house, he says, and even stay overnight in it if you'll arrange in advance. The address is R.F.D. 2, Lincoln, Massachusetts 01773, and the telephone number is 617-259-8709.

IT CHANGED MY WAY OF LOOKING AT THINGS

What you read in a book can be a surprise, an eye-opener, a reason for changing your mind, a new way of looking at life, a basis for espousing a new philosophy.

Many of our interviewees identified this new approach to life as the difference their books made. The first example comes from a man who discovered that brains alone aren't enough.

Dr. Timothy Johnson is a doctor you can understand. He very well may be the best in the country at translating medical terms so all the rest of us can comprehend.

He edits the Harvard Medical School Health Letter to which more than 300,000 subscribe, writes a daily nationally syndicated "House Call" medical column, and conducts an "Update on Health" television program.

His book is *The Best and the Brightest* by David Halberstam, an analysis of the decision-making process that got the United States into the Vietnam War and of the men who made the critical decisions.

"It really opened my eyes in a new way to the fact that simply accumulating the brightest and supposedly best people of our country did not guarantee that we would do the right and moral thing. It was a shocker and eye-opener for me in terms of the fact that every bit as important as intellectual prowess is sort of a moral instinct and judgment of what this country does.

"It made me more realistic, less naive about what it takes to accomplish something good on behalf of our country. Before reading this book, I would have accepted the judgment that if one simply went out and collected the best products of the Eastern Establishment or any other establishment and put them together, then one would have the best result.

"Now I'm less certain about that. I think we need to be every bit as concerned about character and the moral judgment of the people we choose as leaders as we are about their intellectual capacity."

(Timothy Johnson readers may not be aware that before he became a physician, he was in the ministry. He was graduated in 1963 from North Park Seminary, and not until two years later did he enter medical school. Even now he is associate minister of the Community Covenant Church in West Peabody, Massachusetts, and is chairman of the Board of Trustees of North Park College and Theological Seminary.)

More than a million children a year are incarcerated in the United States, either in hospitals, detention homes, reformatories, or adult prisons. More than half of these never have even been accused of a crime. Another 300,000 are locked up for what are called "status offenses"—crimes for which adults cannot be prosecuted, such as playing hooky from school.

Alex Lazzarino is an attorney for the Menninger foundation in Topeka, Kansas, and his job is to find alternative placements—group homes—for children like these who are caught up in the often grim juvenile justice system. His program goes by the acronym CHARLEE —Children Have All Rights, Legal, Educational, Emotional. Thirty of the hoped-for five hundred homes were open by late 1980, and their recidivism rate, Lazzarino said, was only 12 percent in contrast to that of the detention homes and jails, which is a ghastly 90 percent.

His book? Franz Kafka's *Amerika*, the adventures of a young boy who has been driven out of his home by his parents.

"*Amerika* showed me for the first time how humor can be incorporated in a dreadful experience. It taught me that nothing is really as bad as it seems, that there's something funny to be found in everything we do, in everything we're faced with. Before I read it, I was taking myself too seriously."

Babbitt by Sinclair Lewis, is a satire on middle-class life, symbolized by an average American, George F. Babbitt, successful real estate man, regular fellow, booster. David McKean, director of the New Orleans Public Library Jambalaya project financed by a National Endowment for the Humanities grant read it:

"I sort of grew up in the Irish channel here, kind of the working class district. At age seventeen, suburbia looked to me like Nirvana. Then I read *Babbitt*, and for the first time called into question some of the basic outlooks of middle-class life. From my working-class perspective, middle-class life always had seemed an ideal, but after that book, I didn't want to be an accountant any more. It really made me question the American dream, and that meant some growing up for me."

41

A book can be a friend, and something told Linda Scarbro that one particular writer knew and understood.

"The words in his poems were so true," she remembers. "I thought to myself, 'The man who wrote those poems knows what it's like to hurt, to be lonely and unhappy. He knows just how I feel.' "

She was in the third grade. The assignment was to memorize two short poems and recite them to the class. Hers were by American poet Robert Frost—"Lodged" and "Bereft." In each, Frost wrote about "things going bad" and loneliness.

"That was me," Linda recalls. "My life was miserable. I don't remember ever being happy as a child. I coped by saying to myself, 'If I don't think about it, it'll go away.' But it didn't."

And then it was time to stand up in front of everyone. She got through the first poem, then into "Bereft."

> *Something sinister in the tone*
> *Told me my secret must be known . . .*

The tears started. Her secret was that loneliness and no close friends with whom to share. ("I felt ugly as a child. And I was so very shy; I was the one all by myself over in the corner of the playground.")

> *Word I was in the house alone*
> *Somehow must have gotten abroad . . .*

Linda's home was in "one of those West Virginia hollers you read about," deep in the poverty-stricken Appalachian hills. She lived with her grandfather, all his life a coal miner, and her grandmother, weary after rearing eight children of her own. The one-room elementary school was a mile's walk down the hill and across the creek.

Then to the final two lines:

> *Word I was in my life alone,*
> *Word I had no one left but God.*

"They brought out the hurt, all the rejection, right to the surface. I cried so hard I couldn't go on." And she ran out of school and all the way home.

Memories of her childhood still hurt, but Linda recognizes that those poems "opened my eyes to the fact that I was keeping a lot locked up inside me. It did help, though, to understand that I wasn't the only one in the world who was hurting so much."

42

She read more of Frost and then other books, and "came to realize I didn't have to stay in Appalachia and be ignorant."

At age nineteen, she took all the money she had to the Greyhound bus station in Oak Hill, West Virginia, plunked it down on the counter, and asked:

"How far will this take me?"

She'd never been outside West Virginia, and rarely more than fifteen miles from home. But all day on the bus took her to Mansfield, Ohio. There she found friends, a job selling newspaper advertising, a husband and the first happy years of her life.

A better life for her own three children is her dream. "Now I want to take time to let my children know I love them for what they are, not for what I want them to be. To let them know they are wanted and are important to me. To teach them it's OK to say out loud 'I'm sad today'—all things I never had or was permitted to do."

When the family moved to Pine Island, Florida three years ago, Linda Scarbro Letizia became the first director of the Senior Friendship Center on Orange Grove Boulevard in North Ft. Myers. As she built the program and enrolled five thousand members, she recognized much loneliness in the over-sixty set.

"They come here without friends, sometimes without enough money. Many of them lose a spouse. And so many are lonely. That brought back a lot of memories, and took a lot out of me."

Now she's back with a newspaper as a reporter, but the phone still rings. "I must have a pretty good ear, because some of my seniors bend it almost every day."

Robert Frost poems remained her favorites. "The Road Not Taken," for instance, with its famous closing lines:

> *Two roads diverged in a wood, and I—*
> *I took the one less traveled by,*
> *And that has made all the difference.*

The haunting last stanza of "Stopping by Woods on a Snowy Evening":

> *The woods are lovely, dark, and deep,*
> *But I have promises to keep,*
> *And miles to go before I sleep,*
> *And miles to go before I sleep.*

Plus "Mending Wall," with its memorable line *good fences make good neighbors*.

"The more I read Frost, the more I liked him," Linda declares. "He became almost a personal friend. You could look at his picture, look into his eyes, and know he understood.

"I consider his writing a gift. He's given me a part of himself."

***

Life Goes to War: A Picture History of World War II made the difference for Bob Benton, thirty-four years a hotel doorman in Dallas, Texas, now wearing the top hat uniform of the Dallas Sheraton:

"It showed me how we had a lot of suffering that should be worked out some way other than war. It changed me toward human beings. I don't get as upset with them. You may have violent thoughts at times, but you see something like this book, and you say, 'I'd hate to be a part of that,' and then you live more gently."

***

Dan Fader, University of Michigan English professor and author of *Hooked on Books* and *The Naked Children*, said he had to name two books.

The first: Ralph Ellison's *Invisible Man*, about Negro-white relations in the depression decade.

"I spent most of the sixties working with brown and black youngsters in several large cities in large part because Ralph Ellison's book let me know what invisibility meant, let me know the burden of cause, if not of guilt, that we who lived unknowing of invisibility bore. I think I felt responsible, not for where we were but for changing where we were. I spent most of that decade in prisons and reform schools in inner cities trying to understand what it might be like to be a member of a true underclass and to perceive oneself as an underclass, to understand that not only were you in an unhospitable world, but very often if you were in a black underclass, you were in an actively hostile world, especially of the black middle class."

The Second: Dostoyevsky's *The Idiot*, the story of Prince Myskin, rescued from epilepsy and idiocy, who cannot endure the mad world.

"There was another effect, entirely, of *The Idiot*. The character of Prince Myskin in a world obviously not fit for him forced open for me ideas about human psychology and therapeutic media and what the book and words could be to people who were misfit and malfit in society."

***

The *Odyssey* by Homer, a Greek poem relating ten years of wanderings by Odysseus on his way home after the fall of Troy. For Mary Ann Taliaferro, newspaper reporter, Laramie, Wyoming:

"I caught the importance of the individual relying on himself to get out of difficulties. It changed my attitude toward depending on the state to solve everything for me."

Gulliver's Travels by Jonathan Swift, a satire in which an Englishman voyages to imaginary lands. For Professor Edwin McMillan, University of California—Berkeley physicist and 1951 Nobel Prize Laureate for discoveries in the trans-uranium elements:

"In Swift, everything is based on some political fact. It's all satire, just the most brutal stuff imaginable. I had been brought up in what was basically an idealistic family, very protected, and it made me see what the real world was like, gave me a feeling about the seriousness of things."

Main Currents in American Thought by Vernon Louis Parrington, a literary history discussing influential American writers. For William Asp, state librarian of Minnesota:

"That was the first time I'd come across the notion that the proper way to view the history of a country was to view the ideas and beliefs the people hold. It's those ideas that really save all the organizations and institutions society creates. It was a real eye-opener: history through ideas instead of through facts.

"It taught me in working with people that I have to pay a tremendous amount of attention to their beliefs and attitudes and ideas, and that our behavior is determined by our interpretation of our surroundings, of the people around us. It's something I keep in mind when I'm working with state legislators or government officials or anybody."

Cry, the Beloved Country by Alan Paton, a novel of life in South Africa showing the tragic plight of black-skinned people in a white man's world. For Art Brown, manager of mining operations for the Hecla Mining Company in Wallace, Idaho:

"I'm a South African and a staunch believer in most of their principles, but I never could completely agree with apartheid. I read this book, and eventually I left home. I left South Africa and became a U.S. citizen."

Susan Stamberg is co-anchor for "All Things Considered" on National Public Radio in Washington, D.C.

When she was seventeen and a student in the New York City

High School of Music and Art, she read *Black Like Me* by John H. Griffin and *The Autobiography of Malcolm X*. In his book, Griffin describes what happened when he blackened his skin with pigment and travelled through the Deep South masquerading as a Negro. As told to Alex Haley, *Malcolm X* is the story of racism made clear through the life of one man.

"They took a middle-class, New York City girl at a crucial time in the history of the country and opened my eyes to realities that were not immediately apparent to me in my rather privileged life, and at a rather privileged time.

"They've given me a kind of sensitivity and appreciation of the range of human experience I hadn't known before and sensitized me to an enormous segment of the population that was not being appropriately considered or adequately taken care of or carefully thought of."

Ruth J. Boorstin, author, Washington, D.C. picked *The Trial*, by Kafka, an allegory in which a bank clerk leading an inoffensive life is arrested without cause, tries to defend himself, and finally gives up his struggle against authority.

"It objectifies and makes vivid the dilemma we're all in, that we're all in a losing battle, and it's impossible to win, and yet we must win and come to some understanding. It became a way of my facing problems and questions that we all have.

"I read it during the war, during the forties, and it was a picture of the totalitarian world where we have no control, where we're caught in the toils of this monster. We are going to be condemned, and the same person who is the prosecutor also is the judge.

"Today, it helps me get a handle on our computer world. If you've ever tried to struggle with a department store about an error in a computer bill, you know that sense of helplessness."

General Roland Heiser, former commander of U.S. forces in Iran, now director of development, New College, Sarasota, Florida:

"For me, the greatest difference comes from reading history. Too many Americans tend to forget the lessons of history, the way events are related to other events. When something happens in Afghanistan, it's not in isolation, it's related to happenings elsewhere. With a background in history, one can interpret and understand better what goes on today."

John Alfred Hannah was known to more than thirty years of graduates as the president who turned Michigan State from a small "cow college" into one of the nation's major universities.

But John Hannah did more than that. He left the campus and went to Washington. There, as administrator of the United States AID program, he supervised the placement of $22 billion worth of American assistance to the have-not countries around the globe.

With that program, and with the shifts he made in it from an emphasis on guns to agriculture, John Hannah literally changed the world.

And it all came about because of the book that made the greatest difference in his life.

The son of a Grand Rapids, Michigan florist, Hannah at the age of sixteen was secretary of the state poultry society. At twenty-two, he was graduated from the old Michigan State College and started a career as an extension agent. He administered the federal poultry program under the National Industrial Recovery Act of the mid-1930s, then went back to be secretary of the board of trustees and finally president of Michigan State. He left the campus in 1968 to go to Washington.

After four years with AID, he became deputy director of the United Nations to head its World Food Council, where again he supervised a billion-dollar program of food aid for the people of starving nations.

His concern for the poor people of the world began before he became MSU president. He was single in those days, he remembers, and "I didn't have a very broad academic education, but I did have a great deal of interest in the world and in the history of civilization.

"Somewhere, I came across this book by Nehru, the leader of India, written while the British had him locked up in prison. It was *Letters from a Father to His Daughter*, 'a rambling account of history for young people.' " There were 196 letters and 933 pages written to his daughter, Indira, when she was about eleven years old.

"So I bought this great big thick thing, and it was a little like reading a physics book. But it was the first time I had seen a history of people of the world written not from the point of view of a white man.

"It widened my horizon and understanding and my attitude toward non-whites and really made me totally aware that the Chinese and Persians and the ancestors of the people in India had pretty distinguished backgrounds and knew a lot more than I had thought they did.

"Many times since then I have tried to figure out what made it possible for me to become interested in black people or poor people around the world or little people anywhere. There was something in the way of osmosis, or something psychological, that happened to me as a result of reading that book that changed the nature of my interest in the world."

This background helped him lead Michigan State into great international activity; it was the first major U.S. university to have a dean of international programs.

Hannah also headed the U.S. Civil Rights Commission under Presidents Kennedy, Johnson, and Nixon, aiming a relentless spotlight on the grim realities endured by racial minorities in our nation.

In Washington on the AID assignment, Hannah found the Nehru book a benefit in an additional way.

"It was in the late 1960s, when India was in the doghouse in Washington and the State Department. Mr. Rogers, Secretary of State, hated Mrs. Indira Gandhi, India's prime minister, and President Nixon disliked her intensely, extremely.

"Of course, I knew enough about the subcontinent and the importance it played in the world. Also, there were five agricultural universities in India that were built with AID help, and they'd made a great deal of difference to the country.

"Mrs. Gandhi was coming to Washington, and since the President wasn't going to entertain her, and Secretary Rogers wasn't going to entertain her, it fell to my lot as the second man in the State Department to set up a luncheon for her on the top floor of our building.

"She knew she was being given short shrift, but one of the things I mentioned to her was her father's book that I had read, and that pleased her.

"Not too much later, I went over to look at our AID programs in India, and she spent quite a lot of time with me. Ordinarily she was quite perfunctory, but this day she took me in and we chatted about everything under the sun. Then her son who was flying a plane for Air India took some of our party and me to look at some of those universities we'd help start.

"She and I didn't have a really warm, personal friendship, but it was much more than the usual treatment. And for the next several years, I became the defender of the cause of the subcontinent—a very unpopular position at the State Department at that time."

Hannah found the Nehru book because when he was young,

48

"for a good many years I made it a practice to read a book I thought I *ought* to read, not a novel or something I was interested in, every week.

"I knew I wasn't going on academically, but I didn't know what my future was going to be. I didn't have any idea then I was going to spend the rest of my life as a university president, but I do know I read omnivorously.

"I believe what I often said later, that there are many ways of getting an education. Lazy men do best in classrooms and libraries and laboratories, but you can learn just as much if you go through life with your eyes and ears open and your mouth shut, with an inquiring mind, and try to understand what you read and what you hear."

––––––––

Much theory is related to reality, Dan Huntington Fenn, Jr., discovered when he read *A History of Political Theory* by George Holland Sabine in college when he came back from World War II. This college textbook covers the history of political science from Plato and Aristotle to Lenin and Mussolini.

"That made a dramatic change in my thinking about the relationship between theory and philosophy and actual events. It made me realize that theory is not, as I had seemed to think, completely disembodied and cerebral and consequently not very interesting or very relevant, but much more an attempt to abstract from, to generalize about real events, real people, real relationships."

Dr. Fenn, once a staff assistant to President Kennedy in the White House, has been director of the John F. Kennedy Memorial Library in Waltham, Massachusetts since 1971.

––––––––

Ellen Crowley, Wyoming's first woman assistant attorney general, was a state representative in Cheyenne running for her fourth term when we met. Her book was *The Little Prince* by Antoine de Saint-Exupéry, a story of a world of simplicity and beauty with verities for adults as well as children.

"I was introduced to *The Little Prince* while I was in New York going to law school at night, working full-time days in the law library. My father wrote, 'Ellen, why do you do this to yourself?' And about the same time, the wife of the senior law partner for whom I worked said, 'Ellen, I want you to read *The Little Prince*.'

"I did, and *The Little Prince* makes you stop to think. Are you really living, where are you going, what really is important in your life?

"I'm at the stage again where I have to reconstruct my goals, reconstruct my life. But it can't be until after March because I want to win the election again and be a representative for the fourth term, my seventh and eight years, and then I'll have to stop and think what I'm going to do."

(She did win, too.)

Mark Couchman, in the dairy business with his father in Modesto, California, was down in the Grand Canyon when we met.

His book is *The Monkey Wrench Gang* by Edward Abbey.

"Abbey is a very anti-development, anti-tourist, anti-everything we're here for. *The Monkey Wrench Gang* is about four people who get together and go around blowing up bridges and trying to return the desert to its natural condition.

"It gave me a very different outlook. I think too often we get caught up in our own civilization and forget about what the world really is without man. There's so much beauty here that shouldn't be spoiled."

He can represent the little people, the disadvantaged, better because of his book, the former governor of Michigan says.

William G. Milliken served as chief executive longer than any other person in Michigan history. In 1978 he was named by his fellow governors as the most influential governor in the U.S.

His book is by a former professor of his who became president of Yale University, A. Whitney Griswold, and it's *Liberal Education and the Democratic Ideal*, describing liberal education's role as "the legitimate engine of government."

"It has given me a more empathetic understanding of problems and the relationship of problems to people. It applies to everyone but more to people who are disadvantaged, who have not had opportunity, who find themselves caught in a vast governmental and bureaucratic and economic system which they sometimes cannot understand or explain."

Said Stanley Marcus, president emeritus of the Neiman-Marcus department store, Dallas, Texas, and author of *Minding the Store* and *Quest for the Best*:

"It was *Folkways* by William Sumner, a Yale professor of anthropology, which I read after Professor John Livingston Lowe referred to it in his course on poetry."

Folkways defines the ways people satisfy their needs—ways which become habitual and eventually become rules of life policy.

"What that book did for me was sort of open new doors into new horizons of the history of humanity, of the human race. It taught me the important word which he more or less brough⁺ into common usage, the word *mores*.

"It made me recognize that there are more than one or two ways of doing anything in life, and the way that the aborigine in Australia might do a commonplace thing was good for him even though we considered it bad.

"Throughout my adult life, I've maintained an interest in archaeology and anthropology purely as an amateur, but now I'm married to a woman who is studying to get her Ph.D. in archaeology. So the book has made me much more understanding of her work, as well as giving me a better understanding of the world."

Maybe you don't "go around just once." Maybe there really is a second chance.

Nathan Lablang, an architect in Baltimore, Maryland, believes there is.

His book is *The Road Less Traveled* by Morgan Scott Peck, which brings together psychology and religion for readers attempting to integrate personal growth with spiritual search.

"Until I read *The Road Less Traveled*, and even though architecture on the surface appears to be very socially worthwhile, I was involved in it more for ego gratification than for anything else or for anything to do with anyone else's needs.

"After the Peck book, it occurred to me it was time now to put away those totally self-oriented features. It was like getting a second time around. Using what I know in real service, no longer so self-oriented, I'm happier, calmer, understanding more clearly what I should be doing here, not so frenetic, not so hassled. And the income hasn't gone down, either."

Thousands of feet underground, Mark Grubham is a diamond driller in the Hecla Mine at Wallace, Idaho, which bills itself as the silver mining capital of the world.

He's been in the mines for nineteen years, and for the past two also has been president of the miners union, United Steelworkers of America, Local 5514.

His books are histories of the mine and mill union of the steel-workers union.

"They made me more conscious of the labor struggles in history, what labor went through. But they also taught me to see both sides of the story instead of just one.

"Before I read those books I'd been seeing mainly the working man's side; that's where I had been. But after reading those books, I understand you got to look at both sides. You got to be fair. And even though you have personal feelings, there's always two things to look at, and that means theirs as well as yours."

John Gardner, educator, former foundation head, founder of Common Cause:

"The essays of Montaigne reached me early when I was about twenty or twenty-one and had the most widening effect, broadening effect, stimulating effect.

"To understate the thing, what someone called the 'burden of the past' rested very lightly on the shoulders of Californians who grew up in my era. We were not surrounded by an atmosphere of history; the present was very real. The future was almost more real. We just didn't pay much attention to history.

"I was not uninformed on the subject, but I still lacked a sense of the past and for me, Montaigne opened that door. A lot of people get their strongest sense of the past from things that are curious, that are quaint, that have an antique flavor. To me, Montaigne brought the past alive for just the opposite reasons. He seemed so contemporary—a sixteenth century Frenchman who spoke to me as though he were a wise contemporary. It was a revelation that a span of four hundred years could make so little difference.

"There are some really extraordinary things about that man. For instance, his detachment. He lived in a time of great public conflict, but he said of his home, 'I endeavor to free this corner from the public storm as I do another corner of my soul.' You could see that he was writing from that corner of his soul that he had freed.

"He said, 'We're born to search after truth, but not to find it, necessarily. To possess it belongs to a greater power. The question is not who shall win but who shall run the best course.' That's the theme that's run over and over again in my own writing, and I haven't any doubt but my introduction to it was Montaigne."

Bruce Dixon was a Marine Corps radio operator in Vietnam in

1963, handling communications for U.S. generals. His friend told him about Ayn Rand's novel supporting individualism and attacking humanitarianism, *Atlas Shrugged*, and he stayed up three straight nights to finish it.

"Everyone needs some kind of framework to get a start on, especially if you don't have a good religious foundation—which I didn't have," he declares. "This book gave me a lot of direction in organizing my thoughts about politics and economics.

"It's given me a focus, a cultural focus for the way I look at things around me. It explained why the individual is all-important, is more important than the group, and why altruism is not always the answer to things."

Dixon was twenty-three then and says he's moderated some of those views since then. Today's he's a news and feature broadcaster for public radio station WBFO in Buffalo, N.Y.

———

Hubert Davis, Portsmouth, Va., retired schoolteacher, principal, and superintendent, named *Julius Caesar* by William Shakespeare.

"I came from down in the mountains in western Virginia where you couldn't see over the treetops, so this book gave me a wider horizon. In fact, I never knew there were places called England or London until I read that book as a sophomore in high school.

"The beautiful language Shakespeare used was similar to the language I was accustomed to in the mountains, because we were descended from the Elizabethan period Scotch-Irish people."

Mr. Davis has had five recent books published and is president of the trustees section of the Virginia Library Association. He's seventy-eight.

———

Emily Post's *Etiquette* made the difference for Jean Sapp, now a mother and housewife in Chatmoss, Va. "When I was just a girl, it was required reading before I could go anywhere. If I was invited to a friend's for dinner, my mother would turn to the appropriate chapter and say this is what I had to read before I had permission to go there. What a thoughtful mother she was—I grew up knowing how to be polite in public."

———

What matters in understanding something—in history or politics or your own life—"is not what you may emotionally want to believe, but what can be gleaned from the pluses and minuses on all sides."

That's Michael Welch speaking, and he's referring to what he learned from *The Rising Sun: The Decline and Fall of the Japanese Empire* by John Toland.

"It taught me that even our surest beliefs about our national past can be challenged.

"To be mature about this country's history or any morality in general," he continues, "one must know that the good guys are not always good nor are the bad guys always bad."

That book is a history of the Japanese Empire from 1936 to 1945, and "makes one think beyond cliches, and understand that no one is really entirely right or entirely wrong."

Welch is a line worker at the Heileman Brewing company plant in LaCrosse, Wis., and lives across the Mississippi in Hokah, Minnesota.

Manchild in the Promised Land by Claude Brown "was an eye-opener for a middle-class white college freshman from a California suburb," David Wright, New York City free-lance advertising and public relations writer, reported.

The book is a dramatic autobiography of one man and, at the same time, of millions of slum-imprisoned Negroes.

"It shook me loose from the time and place I grew up in. Reading this very vivid account of life in an urban black environment made me realize that so much that is human is universal. It showed me that love and beauty and excitement and integrity flourished in places I never dreamed of. After that, no fellow human could ever be wholly an 'object,' whether of respect and admiration or of fear and revulsion."

WHAT IS WRONG WITH A WOMAN
WANTING TO MAKE MONEY?

In the spacious governor's mansion of Colorado, the wife of the governor speaks about thoughts and feelings and emotions that could be Everywoman's.

For Dottie Lamm, the book is *Working It Out*, edited by Sara Ruddick and Pamela Daniels, the true stories of how twenty-three women managed to keep a creative work life going.

"It came at a time in my life when I was really needing to struggle with what kind of career I was going to turn to. Being the governor's wife and being the mother of the children was not really enough emotional satisfaction, although some people would say, 'My Lord, that is all any woman could need.'

"That was part of the problem. All along women have been told that that's all any woman could need. The fact is that work is just as important for women as it is for men.

"One reason is creativity. Another is money. What is wrong with a woman wanting to make money?"

Women always have worked, Mrs. Lamm says, and "homemakers work harder than anyone else. So I do not mean to say homemakers are not workers.

"What I am saying is that it gave me more courage to carve out a personal area of work that was both paid and more satisfying to me than to do some of the kinds of work you get into that are connected with a family, like volunteer work and that sort of thing.

"This book made me decide to insist on being paid, not to feel guilty if it interfered with being chairwoman of this committee or that committee. I've made work a priority now rather than a kind of second hobby."

What she did was "pull back from volunteerism and try to develop my writing.

"To see if a major newspaper in Colorado would hire me, to see if indeed I could write; that was a big step because most people learn to write before they even approach a big newspaper. And I'd written only something like eight articles when I approached the *Denver Post*."

The real writing, she says, "came because I started writing my personal experiences during my husband's first campaign for governor. I never thought I would publish them, but I wrote them because it, well, it was kind of like I needed somebody to talk to. You're a political wife on the first campaign trip; you don't have time for personal friends any more. And the writing kind of became my friend."

After the election, she read over her diary. "I realized then that this wasn't really a political story, that it was a story about being a wife of someone prominent in either public or private life, and that a lot of women would identify with it. So I had it published in a small Colorado magazine, and the comments I got from that made me decide to go on."

Now she does a Monday editorial page column for the *Post*. "I have a very interesting platform to be on by writing for them, and I get letters based on what I write, not on the fact that I'm the governor's wife."

She writes "things that touch on people's lives, that make them reevaluate their lives." One column described what it's like being the wife of the governor ("second bananas have to spend so much time waiting"). Another on the different salutations for women, especially "Ms.," drew eight hundred responses.

She is paid for the column, and also for being the host of a weekly half-hour public affairs program on which she interviews public figures for the Denver NBC television station.

The money? Here she stops being independent—"it goes into our joint bank account.

"But," she lets you know, "it's enough over the course of a year to pay for our groceries, or for our clothes, or one major item like that."

READING ALSO REINFORCES

One of the major rewards of reading is to find agreement with and reinforcement of your own ideas and attitudes. And if the author also has put into logical order your own half-formed thoughts, how sweet it is!

———

The star curmudgeon of "A Few Minutes with Andy Rooney" on 60 Minutes on CBS television chose Walter Lippmann's *Preface to Morals*, an analysis of the confusion and disillusion of the modern age and an attempt to find a way out through the acceptance of a higher humanism.

"*Preface to Morals* has more philosophy, logic and good sense than anything else I ever read," Rooney said. "I read it in college in 1941, and it made understandable to me a lot of ideas I had only half had. Lippmann managed to crystallize them so I understood what it was I was trying to think."

Time magazine has called Rooney "the most felicitous nonfiction writer in television." He has won the Writers Guild award for the best script of the year six times, more than any other writer in the history of television.

———

An escaped slave who never had a day of formal school wrote the autobiography that inspired William Branch, a much honored black playwright and professor, to become a writer.

The book was *The Life and Times of Frederick Douglass*. It recounted his early life as a slave, his escape, then his steady influence on public opinion that helped urge President Lincoln's Emancipation Proclamation freeing the slaves.

Son of an African Methodist Zion Church minister, Bill Branch knew his share of discrimination.

In North Carolina, "there was that separate-but-equal facilities law. There was great emphasis on the separate and none at all on the equal." Even the library was segregated.

In Washington, D.C. he was the first black to win the district-wide American Legion oratorical contest. But the first newspaper accounts included a picture of the American Legion official congratulating the *second place* winner—a white youth.

He won a four-year, all-expenses college scholarship, and chose to attend Northwestern University, just outside Chicago. But even there, in 1945, blacks were not permitted to live in campus dormitories, so he had to stay in the YMCA—the segregated branch, that is.

He wanted to become an actor but found almost no roles for Negroes other than "dese, dem, and dose" parts for servants. So he wrote his own, and a string of prize-winning plays and television and film scripts followed. *A Model for Willie* still is being performed on the stage today. *In Splendid Error*, about Frederick Douglass and abolitionist John Brown of Harper's Ferry fame, had an off-Broadway run to critical acclaim.

Today Branch is a visiting professor of Afro-American Studies at the Baltimore campus of the University of Maryland. He teaches literature and drama and conducts a theatre workshop.

For his plays and television scripts, he has won a Columbia University award, a John Simon Guggenheim fellowship, a blue ribbon award from the American Film Festival, an Emmy nomination from the National Academy of Television Arts and Sciences, and the Robert E. Sherwood television award.

Young Bill Branch grew up determined "never to compromise with racism." The Douglass book reinforced that resolve.

"But the fight today is even harder than before the Supreme Court decision prohibiting segregation and saying that separate-but-equal thing did not work, back in the 1950s," Branch declares. "Today, so much of the discrimination is underground."

Within this, how does a black man survive, how does he cope? In answer, Branch quotes parts of an 1849 letter in which Frederick Douglass sees human liberty won only after a struggle:

"If there is no struggle, there is no progress.

"Those who profess to favor freedom and yet depreciate agitation are men who want crops without plowing, rain without thunder and lightning.

"Power concedes nothing without a demand.

"Find out just what people will submit to, and you have found out the exact amount of injustice and wrong which will be imposed upon them, and these will continue until they are resisted with either words or blows or both.

"The limits of tyranny are prescribed by the endurance of those whom they oppress.

"Men may not get all they pay for in this world, but they most certainly pay for all they get."

————

Dorothy Moeller, Iowa City, Iowa journalist and author, named *Walden* by Thoreau.

"It reinforces and makes decent my feeling about fundamentals in nature. It was the support of the written word for something I had felt, a legitimizing. Things I had known but never really known, that nature does speak to you and is to be listened to, and that in silence, in quiet and simplicity, there is virtue, there is value, there is a message."

————

In his office as football coach emeritus at Ohio State University, Woodrow Wayne Hayes named Ralph Waldo Emerson's essay, "Compensation."

"It says there's always two sides, always the other side of the coin. For every good thing there's a bad one; for all lightness, there's dark. When you start looking at anything you do, you must consider the consequences. For example:

"In coaching big-time football, I never got into any scandals, I never had any big problems with youngsters because of one thing: I was going to wring all the football from them I could get, and I did. (We had more All-Americans than anybody else. We've had more in professional football than anybody else.) We're going to get all the football out of the youngster, but what is he going to get in return?

"What he'll get in return is the opportunity for the best education he can get in college, and the person who can make sure he doesn't shirk that, because lots of kids will overlook that part, the one who can do that better than anyone else is the head football coach.

"There's been no football coach in this country who's spent more time at the study table with his football players than Woody

Hayes has. And if Woody Hayes sets the example, the other coaches will follow and the players will be there.

"It all comes back to the inevitable question: If you're going to utilize a man, what are you going to give him in return? That's what I learned from that book."

Mao Tse-tung wrote it. Clara Garcia remembers it well.

"I left it right there on the bookshelf in the living room. After all, I had read it, I had understood it, I had decided to leave my homeland because of it."

Mrs. Garcia was one of the first wave of immigrants from Cuba to the United States back in the early 1960s. She had been a professor on the faculty of the teacher's college, and her husband had been a captain in the military (but "retired" at 36 because he didn't agree politically with the country's new ruler, Fidel Castro).

The book was one of about twenty supplied to each faculty member in the college. They were all about what to expect from Castro and Communism. The particular one that convinced Mrs. Garcia to leave Cuba was by the Chinese leader on *The School of Work*.

"It told about how the students in China were in the classroom four hours a day and then out in the fields four hours a day. It confirmed what we knew we could expect from Castro. This was notice being given to us. So we left everything behind and came here."

In Cuba they'd been relatively well-to-do. Moving to freedom meant considerable sacrifice. Mr. Garcia's first job was as a Good Humor ice cream man. Hers was in hand embroidery. Eventually they moved to Union City, New Jersey. Mrs. Garcia, now a widow, teaches Spanish to English-speaking students in high school there.

Nineteen Eighty-Four is a satirical novel about a time (far in the future when the book was written in 1949), when people living in a collectivist society are persuaded by Thought Police that ignorance is strength and war is peace. For Phil Samson, utility man, bumper assembly line, Oldsmobile Cutlass automobile plant, Lansing, Michigan:

"It made me realize how lucky we are to live in this country and have the freedom we have. I don't think the people would put up with that kind of complete government control in this country. In Russia that's all they've ever known, but the people in America know what freedom is. It made me sure I'd never give it up."

Mortimer Adler, philosopher, author, director of the Institute for Philosophical Research, University of Chicago, and chairman of the Board of Editors of the *Encyclopaedia Britannica*, answers his own office telephone at 7:30 in the morning, and makes things clear in a hurry.

Aristotle's *Ethics*, he said. Aristotle believed that a man who has difficulty behaving ethically is morally imperfect, that moral virtue is a matter of avoiding extremes in behavior.

"I understood through that book and through no other what it means to say we're engaged in the pursuit of happiness."

For Arthur Eastman, Blacksburg, Virginia, head of the Virginia Tech department of English and general editor of *The Norton Reader* used by almost a million college and university students since 1964, it's another work by Aristotle, the *Poetics*. In it, Aristotle examines how tragedy deeply affects the spectator by arousing pity and fear and then purifying and cleansing him of these emotions.

"I first read this in a class in Literature of the Western World that Hutchins and Adler were trying out on students in the University of Chicago laboratory school. In college, I read it several more times, and it began to get through to me that here was a way of thinking about things, about means relating to ends, about forms fulfilling functions, that I've found governing my thought about almost all problems ever since."

Johnny Got His Gun by Dalton Trumbo, deals with the thoughts of a terribly maimed soldier living in a hospital, his gradual realization of his condition, and his hopes of communication with those around him. For Kerry Drake, editor of the Sunday *Tribune-Eagle*, Cheyenne, Wyoming:

"I read this while in high school, approaching draft age, and it made the horror of war more real even than when we sat in a classroom and talked about it. It was the first time, so powerful and descriptive, it really sank in."

Lord of the Flies by William Golding, in which English school boys, ages six to twelve, stranded on a uninhabited island, manage for themselves in a fight between civilization and barbarism, affected Ron Dubberly, public librarian of Seattle, Washington:

"It strengthened my feelings that not only do our cultural institutions make us more civilized but also that they are necessary to have in a free society so we do not succumb to a dictatorship."

The dean of geology and mines at the University of Idaho, Malcolm Maynard Miller, names the four-page essay by Ralph Waldo Emerson, "The American Scholar," in which Emerson advises his audience to read the great book of nature.

"The universal truths in that essay struck home, especially the part about the greatest teacher we will ever know, which of course is nature.

"I've found that nature obscures truth in a vicious, bitchy way. You've got to put your ear to the ground to read nature because nature speaks so softly.

"Nature also speaks in a foreign language, and we have to learn that language, that physics or chemistry or geology or metallurgy or whatever. And it often lisps so that you can't read through it unless you understand that lisp."

The temperature had topped one hundred degrees Fahrenheit for something like eleven days in a row the Sunday morning we took the first boat out into the Charleston, South Carolina harbor to the Fort Sumter National Monument.

This is the place that suffered the first shots fired in the Civil War. Tourists learn about it from a couple of National Park Service technicians, one man wearing—despite the heat—the heavy wool uniform of a Federal soldier of 1861.

Now thirty-two, Bob Hart remembered the book he'd read at age eleven—*The Age of Reason* by Thomas Paine, whose views on religion disagreed with many accepted church teachings of his time.

"It gave me a certain skepticism about the establishment, things that are established. And that's run my whole life."

Hart is a graduate of the Air Force Academy, but after seven years in service, resigned. Then he was a graduate student in archaeology, from which he also resigned (this time to marry another "arch" major he'd met). He's been telling tourists about Fort Sumter for two years; that won't last forever either, he says.

He sits high in the John Hancock building in Boston in a corner office and is president of the seven companies that form the advisers group for the hundreds of millions of dollars of investments in John Hancock Mutual Funds.

His book actually is forty volumes he read ("as a diversion") during Harvard days—the testimony in the post World War II war criminal trials at Nuremberg.

"They convinced me that authority should always be questioned, always put on its mettle," Bruce Oliver said. "If we don't, we end up with a mess like Hitler's."

___

One authority, however, received resounding support. It was chosen as having made the greatest difference by almost five out of every one hundred persons we interviewed—but what a wide variety of differences they testified it had made!

"THE MOST POWERFUL SINGLE VOLUME YOU ENCOUNTER"

All sorts of people made the Bible the most-named book in our study—a public leader, a championship golfer, the head of the family about which *The Sound of Music* was made, an editor, a grocery store owner, a novelist, and others.

___

"I don't think you can possibly grow up in an education in which the exposition of the life and the meaning of the life of Jesus is central, and not say that the New Testament is the most important book in your life, however much or little you may have in fact lived by it. It's the most powerful single volume you encounter."

That's McGeorge Bundy talking, the former Harvard dean, the former special assistant for national affairs to Presidents Kennedy and Johnson, the former president of the Ford Foundation. He adds:

"It presents the unattainable standard of decency, or good behavior, or the moral life. Everybody has the problem of living with some kind of notion of what you ought to do, and those are the most powerful notions of 'ought' that I've lived with."

___

"One New Year's Day when I was nine, I made a resolution to read the Bible all the way through, and I did. I'm not a religious fanatic, but that's the first thing I think of for making a difference. There was so much in it worth trying to live by that I did, in fact, adopt the Golden Rule. That gave me a great deal of strength."

—Hazel Dickens-Garcia, professor of journalism, University of Minnesota.

A husband-and-wife team...
Tim Melton, newscaster, WCPO-TV, Cincinnati, Ohio:
"It brought me to a saving knowledge of the Lord Jesus Christ. The manner in which I live my life, the values I have, the judgments I make, the decisions I reach, are based in great part on what is in the Bible."
Nancy Lopez-Melton, professional golfer:
"The first gift Tim ever gave me was a Bible, it was part of his courting. It was very special to me. I was hoping we'd get married, but I never said that to Tim (I knew it before he did).

"When I read the Bible, whether I've had a good day or bad day on the course, it fits into my life. I can put my golf into the Bible and the Bible into my golf. When I lose, I don't say 'God did something bad to me,' because he's been so good to me.

"Tim and I read a part every day and by the end of the year, we've read the whole Bible. When we're apart, we read the same things so we can kind of be in the same thought for that day."

The Baroness Maria von Trapp, of Stowe, Vermont, upon whose family story *The Sound of Music* was based:
"I grew up in Austria and took the Bible for granted, except I didn't read it. It was there, and I was there, but I didn't have any real connection with it.

"I don't remember why, but I do remember how one day when I was in my late twenties, I opened the Bible and was just amazed. I couldn't stop reading. I started in the New Testament, and then went back to the Old, and there I found with growing excitement the answers to all the questions—how it all started, what is the most important thing in life. It is all there.

"It's like a beacon to get your connections from."

A caller to our talk show on WRNG, Atlanta:
"It changed me from a wayward person to one trying to follow in Christ's footsteps and be a Christian."

Loyal Meek, editor, *Phoenix Gazette*:
"There is some awfully good reporting and editorializing in it."

The Rev. Howard Ramsey, head of the personal evangelism department of the Southern Baptist Convention, Home Mission Board, Atlanta:

"In 1956, I was born again. I knew I had really found a direction in my life. Since then, I've adopted the Bible as the absolute authority for life, the way to live life."

Glenn Holliday, director of film, radio, and television, Catholic archdiocese of Denver, Colorado:

"My life has been a coming into awareness of God. In my college years, people began to challenge me to take God seriously, to make decisions, not necessarily to accept everything I'd always been taught about God and my life. That was when I began to look into the Bible in more depth, and my faith was confirmed rather than lost during my college years."

It is just a tiny dot on the border between Missouri and Arkansas, a rather narrow wide place in the road called Blue Eye. There is the Junction Grocery, Feed, and Service Store, and at the cash register is Janice Settles.

For her, it's what the Bible teaches about running the business.

"For instance, we don't raise prices when we don't have to. When there is a notification of a price increase, many places right then raise the prices on what's already in stock that they paid a lower price for. But we don't raise until we actually pay more for the product."

Also the matter of making change.

"There have been times when after a customer leaves, we find we made a mistake and shortchanged him. He doesn't know it, and we wouldn't have to, but we make sure he gets the right change back."

Margaret Walker (Armstrong), Jackson, Mississippi, author of *Jubilee*:

"I had a Bible presented to me as a prize when I was twelve years old for having given an oration on the American Negro's obligation to Africa. That was a very beautiful Bible that came from the divinity school where my father had graduated earlier.

"I read that Bible every day until I was twenty-one years old and I think the rhythms of that Bible appear in my poetry. My first editor, Stephen Vincent Benet, said when he read my poetry that there were Biblical rhythms in it."

Joan Hopkins, county library director, Sarasota, Florida:
"The Bible gave me the morality I deal with in my everyday life."

Norman Morrison, San Diego, California, was resting on his hike part-way down into the Grand Canyon.

The Bible is his book for "the concepts, the precepts, the values that were pounded into me. Heck, I won New Testaments galore for perfect attendance—enforced, of course—and those things were pounded into me, and they helped.

"I've got three kids today who haven't been arrested, all are married for the first time, and all are still married. We must have done something right, and I credit it to the Bible."

The Talmud, the authoritative body of Jewish tradition and that ancient answer to all questions of Jewish law, is the book for Dr. Solomon Freehof, rabbi emeritus of Rodef Shalom Temple in Pittsburgh. He studied it so much "its mode of argument affected my work and became my mode."

He especially used the Talmud when he headed the Jewish division of the chaplaincy for the U.S. armed services in World War II. With it, he answered queries from chaplains in the field and also found the basis for seven of his books.

Rabbi Freehof remembers the very first question the Pentagon forwarded: Inasmuch as Jewish services are at sunset on Friday, when would you have services in a country like Iceland where sunset lasts for six months?

The answer: Trust the Talmud. Written long before Iceland was even settled, it has an answer that can be adapted.

Rabbi Freehof:

"The Talmud says that if a man is traveling in the desert, and the scenery is monotonous, and one day is like another, it dawns on him one day that he has forgotten what day of the week it is. Now he and his camels will be working on the Sabbath without his knowing it—which he cannot do. So he should take the day he thought about this, and call that Sunday, and then six days later will be the Sabbath for him."

(What actually happened during the war was that Jewish servicemen in Iceland observed the same Sabbath as Portland, Maine did, and those in Alaska, that of Portland, Oregon.)

One who named the Bible said that for her, "The Bible means the difference between living a life of despair and hopelessness and a life of joy and hope."

The Psalms give Mrs. Howard Cannon great comfort, "especially that part about making a joyful noise.

"That's what I've lived by, making joyful noises. I'm convinced that Jesus had a magnificent sense of humor—I even have one picture of him with his head thrown back, roaring with laughter at some joke."

When she started her professional career more than forty years ago, she wanted to be a dramatic actress. Instead, "the Lord led me to be something else," and she created the character she's played at the Grand Ole Opry "for the one purpose of bringing joy and happiness to people.

"Now one of the bright spots of my life is that people say to me, over and over, that they have laughed and they have felt a little better from having heard this character. And that's all I ask of my life, of my career, is that people find happiness in Minnie Pearl."

The Bible pops up in places you wouldn't expect it. One was in a bookstore in Seattle, the only place on our interviews Patricia wouldn't accompany me.

I walked in, tape recorder slung over my shoulder, microphone in obvious view, and introduced myself.

The proprietor was behind the counter, cigarette hanging with a long ash.

What book made the greatest difference in your life?

He looked doubtfully toward a customer leaning against the counter, paging through a picture magazine.

"Well, the Bible, I guess."

What was the difference it made?

A half-grin at the customer.

"Well, it teaches you right from wrong."

And how long have you been in this business here?

Whereupon the proprietor of John's Adult Book Store threw me out.

RAY OF HOPE

Her family had grown and she was forty when she enrolled at the University of Iowa as a freshman. Four years later, she was graduated with honors—but not before a shocking incident through which she discovered the book that made the greatest difference to her.

The book was *Beyond Our Selves* by Catherine Marshall, widow of Peter Marshall, the late chaplain of the United States Senate.

"I read this shortly before Bill's death," Elnora Ross said.

"It was during the month we were separated, and he was telephoning and threatening my life and drinking so heavily, and I was in such confusion, such turmoil.

"I wanted this marriage to work, I wanted it to last. I could see what he was doing to himself. I knew what he would do to me if I let him come home, knowing that he was still drinking so heavily, and that as before, I would be hurt physically. He would beat me up again.

"And yet when he was not drinking, the relationship was pure heaven, so I was torn almost completely down the middle, right in half. There was no way. I couldn't even 'fight or flight' because half of me wanted so much what I knew was right, and the other half of me knew that I didn't dare.

"The book helped me to get my mind off of myself—and on to myself. Mrs. Marshall was writing about how she coped with her husband's death, and how her life began to take on a new and different kind of meaning because of the loss, and in a way, I could relate to that. I knew I was experiencing a loss, and because Bill was threatening suicide so much, I knew I had a chance of experiencing that kind of loss.

"In a way, the book helped me through sort of an anticipatory grief, so that I think had I not read this book before Bill's death, I would have probably taken my own life after his death."

Mrs. Ross continued.

"It also gave me a new awareness of God, not just as somebody sitting up there on a throne that's an untouchable, but someone who through the Holy Spirit really does touch the individual and is there for you to draw on for strength.

"That's when I tapped in. That's when I was aware of a reserve force that my faith could draw upon, and so I had this strength in reserve when Bill's suicide came along.

"Without it, his suicide would have destroyed me too."

After that, Mrs. Ross didn't just sit idly. She founded an organization called Ray of Hope as a nonprofit mutual support service to the families and friends of persons who have committed suicide. Its goal is to help them understand what's happened and how they can pick up the pieces and go on living.

"The point of Ray of Hope is to take a tragedy, maybe even generations of tragedy, and turn it into a growth process that provides a ray of hope for everyone," she said.

"Statistics and studies of suicides show that members of their families themselves have an increased risk of suicide and to earlier death by other cause, and to a host of physical, social, financial, psychological, and mental maladaptive behavior that may come along anywhere from a few weeks to even years after the suicide takes place.

"The reason is that society doesn't know how to react to the families, and so they don't react at all.

"The time when the family needs comfort the most is when they receive it the least. As a result, they can't work through a healthy grief process, and there's a tremendous need to find a reason why this death occurred.

"We need to find that reason so we can remove a sense of shame from everyone and restore a sense of dignity to the departed person and a sense of self-worth and identity to ourselves, because suddenly it looks like we let someone down so badly that they chose death. You have to look good again to yourself and in the eyes of the community."

Ray of Hope participation is "open to everyone." Her address is Mrs. Elnora Ross, 1518 Derwen Drive, Iowa City, Iowa 52240. Her telephone number is 319-351-0330.

THEY JUST MAKE YOU FEEL BETTER

Self-confidence, comfort, a release from stress, an appreciation of life, contentment. All these happy states were brought about by the books some people read.

They just made them feel better.

––––––––––

It's love stories for Mrs. Emma Williams Staunton Thompson Simpson, age eighty-one, in the St. Petersburg Florida Convalescent Center.

"I like the romance stories. Not the mushy kind; just the regular everyday ones that turn out all right. They give you a lift, somehow or other."

––––––––––

Science fiction. For Nancy White, assistant director, Spokane, Washington public library:

"I had been going through a particularly stressful period, and the distance that science fiction allowed me to maintain was a very healing kind of quality. I could become totally immersed in fantasy and all the things I had to deal with at work and in personal relationships were gone completely."

Walden by Henry Thoreau. For William Andrews, Swarthmore, Pa., academic dean, Philadelphia College of Textiles and Science:

"It gave me a sense of self-confidence about my own differences from other people."

Everyone has about the same ideas and the same thoughts but at different times.

That's the message *The Sensuous Woman* by J gave to Mary Waller, a Los Angeles talent agency staff member. *The Sensuous Woman* is a how-to book for the female who yearns to be "all woman."

"It made me more comfortable with myself, brought me more into contact with myself. It really helped me relax with other people and know they're thinking the same things I was. After that, it was just a matter of getting our timing together."

Reverdy Mullins' book was the one that made him realize "the gospel isn't the gospel."

He read it in the Aleutian Islands only ninety miles from Kiska, Alaska, to which he flew a P-40 fighter plane two or three times a day to drop bombs and strafe Japanese invaders—and to have them shoot back at him.

When his fighter squadron was hastily ordered to the Aleutians early in World War II, Mullins was in Seattle. He dumped all his clothes out of a footlocker, then filled it with $150 worth of books he frantically grabbed in the bookstore nearest his base.

One book caught his mind.

"I don't remember the name of it or the author, but it was about the origins of religion and comparative religions.

"I had grown up with a reasonable amount of churchgoing, and this book opened my eyes for the first time to the possibility that there could be thoughts about religion other than those I inherited.

"It freed me from the myths and shibboleths and guilt that most organized religions afflict people with.

"I found the common denominator among so many religions, found out there was no exclusive hold either on myths or ethical components. As a result, my life has been totally free of any of the pretensions that usually are imposed on people by their religions.

"It was a great unshackling. All of a sudden, I realized the gospel wasn't the gospel, and why."

After the war, Mullins studied journalism and became a newsman and television entertainer. He now lives in Kansas City, Kansas and is vice-president of Luzier Cosmetics.

Not the Bible but a related secular book made the difference to a beauty shop operator and a professional football star. It is *Late Great Planet Earth*, a conservative Christian view of the Second Coming and the time beyond, by Hal Lindsey and C.C. Carlson.

For Joyce Hull, beauty parlor manager, Cincinnati, Ohio:

"It woke me up to the fact that the end is coming, and I should be prepared spiritually for where I would like to spend eternity. I'm a lot happier after reading it."

And also for D. D. Lewis, a standout linebacker for the Dallas Cowboys professional football team:

"I was brought up in the church but it was like I had to go, so I didn't get a lot out of it, just your basic Sunday-school verses memorized.

"This book got me back into the Bible, reading about things I hadn't read about in a long time. It got me back into a prayer life. To a walk with God. A feeling of a Holy Spirit. The reason Jesus Christ was here, the reason for Christianity. It aligned me with the spirit of God and has given me peace of mind."

Aboard Eastern Airlines flight 116, Phoenix to Atlanta.

Stewardess Jane Diaz, from Annandale, Minnesota, husband a draftsman, been flying nine years, has a young daughter at home.

"It was a calorie book, and did I ever need it. It helped me lose the weight I wanted to lose and made me healthier and feel better about myself when I wanted to come back to work after having that wonderful baby."

Books make a difference to all ages.

Mrs. Mary Regina Weiss Schwab was more than halfway past her 100th toward her 101st birthday anniversary when we talked in the St. Petersburg, Florida Convalescent Center.

"Long life?" she repeated. "I attribute it all to your way of thinking. I've always tried to look on the bright side of things, to do the best I could and be cheerful, no matter what."

She also said she believes in "feeding your mind" and reads every spare moment. Her book was Edna Ferber's *Great Son*, a chronicle of four generations of a Seattle family beginning in 1851 and ending the day of Pearl Harbor. She said it made her "more alert to humanity and to what life could mean."

A caller to our program on WRNG, Atlanta named *I'm OK, You're OK* by Dr. Thomas Harris, a guide to transactional analysis that distinguishes between three active elements in each person's make-up: parent, adult, and child.

"I felt as if it had been written for me, it made that much of an impact.

"It helped me understand exactly what was going on inside me, and where other people are coming from, and why they are acting the way they are.

"It made me so much more tolerant of other people as well as giving me a feeling of self-worth. When I was a youngster, I received so many negative messages, I was programmed so negatively, I never thought much of myself. This book absolutely turned me around."

Grapes of Wrath by John Steinbeck, is the story of the small farmers and sharecroppers of the Southwest driven out of their homes and moving westward with their families and goods. For Coke Gayle, Jr., a theater graduate of the University of Idaho, now a hardware store owner in Moscow, Idaho:

"It made me appreciate the labor movement more and made me thankful for what I have, for the fact that I don't have to fight for it like those folks did."

In New Orleans, after you've eaten well and heard wonderful jazz, what's next?

Perhaps you'd like to visit Pat O'Brien's bar in the French quarter, next door to Preservation Hall. Pat's is an emporium, legend has it, so popular that during Mardi Gras the crowds are so thick and waiting lines so long that a representative of the management shouts "FIRE" once every hour so that all the customers will rush out a back exit and make space for another roomful.

Pat's has two major attractions:

One is the Hurricane, a speciality-of-the-house drink, rum-based and pink, served in a hand-blown hurricane glass which costs you $1.50 extra if you keep it.

The second is a pair of two-piano teams, four energetic women who play nonstop from 8 p.m. to 2 a.m. One of these is Connie Kaye who is New Orleans' veteran entertainer and who has been on the same job for twenty-five years.

Connie Kaye started playing nightclubs and lounges when she was eighteen and had traveled the country over before Pat's beckoned in 1955.

The night we were there, she was bouncing and belting and playing the audience.

But inside it must have been different. For her book, *Peace of Mind* by Rabbi Joshua Liebman, had helped her "find out how to live more peacefully. It made my life easier, gave me a sort of feeling of contentment, sort of tranquilized my life."

Peace of Mind distills insights, about human nature and man's capacity to change and improve, that are correlated with religious insights and goals.

"I walked on cloud nine for weeks after I finished it."

The book is *Love* by Leo Buscaglia, a commentary on the potential of each of us to love and the great amount of love there is all around us.

It made the difference to Gregg Grisa, of Stevens Point, Wisconsin. "It's absolutely the most exhilarating and beautiful book I ever read," he said.

She was a Jewish seventh grader in a German public school just as the Nazis were stepping up their anti-Jewish harassment and ostracism, and "books had become the only world into which I could escape to live free and without fear."

Susan Faulkner found Homer's *Iliad* and *Odyssey*.

"In the *Iliad*, the heroism of the warriors nourished my spirit when I needed heroes, and the description of war's brutalities confirmed my pacifism. In contrast, the *Odyssey* captured my imagination with its tale of the journey of one adventurous, daring individual, a man both hero and fox, back to his beloved Ithaca."

Those two gave her an enduring love for Greek art, history, and philosophy, and "the gorgeous music of the poetry propelled me into literary studies.

"Homer's epics sustained my lonely soul, giving me an inspiring vision of a wide open world I might yet find and much needed strength as well as greater confidence in my own inner resources for my own wanderings to come."

She's now earned the Ph.D., lives in Jackson Heights, N.Y., and is retired from her work as a secretary.

THE DIFFERENCE CAN TAKE PLACE
AT A VERY EARLY AGE

When does reading start to make a difference?

At a very early age, said many of the people we listened to. They were adults when we interviewed them, but our question quickly took them back to childhood days.

The books that made the difference ranged from comics to Shakespeare, from *Heidi* to one about cats. And the difference has stayed with a famous actor, an artist-cartoonist, an author, a businessman, an ambassador, one of the most veteran sailors in the U.S. Navy, a book publishing executive, an airline pilot, an editor, and others.

———

Alan Alda, the movie and television actor and writer, always looks as though he has things well in hand. No doubts, no indecision.

There was a time, though, when he wavered and waffled. When he was very young, it took him three successive books to find the one that finally made the greatest difference. There was:

Top Horse at Crescent Ranch, a children's book.

"I read it when I was eight. I immediately sat down and tried to write my own book about a horse. From then on, I knew I wanted to write."

The Legends of King Arthur, at about age ten.

"I would read myself to sleep at night with the magic of Merlin and the decency and cleverness of the Knights of the Round Table. From then on, I knew I wanted to be a magician."

The Congressional Record.

"For some reason, leatherbound copies of the goings-on in Congress lined the shelves of our living room, and I pored over them when I was twelve. I had never read anything so funny. From then on, I knew I wanted to do comedy."

———

He draws the comic strip "Shoe," which appears in more than five hundred U.S. daily and Sunday newspapers.

And he drew the political cartoons that you saw on many editorial pages and that twice won him the Pulitzer prize.

This double-barreled approach made Jeff MacNelly one of the most successful artist-cartoonists in the business. But it hasn't made him forget the book that made the greatest difference in his life: *Up Front*, a collection of famous cartoonist Bill Mauldin's World War II Willie and Joe Cartoons.

"I read it when I was twelve, and it's the one that got me tickled about the whole concept of cartooning, political cartooning in particular, and especially the way that Mauldin treated humor in the face of stark adversity, of pretty bleak situations.

"This book planted the seed. And it's followed me all along. I still use it, and I have it in my studio at home."

That's in Richmond, Virginia, where MacNelly was on the staff of the *News Leader* for eleven years.

David McCord, poet and author of forty-five books, eleven of them verse for children, whose poems are reprinted in 350 textbooks from London to Australia, the man who has read his poems to more than 100,000 school children, was watching Monday night football on television in the basement of the Harvard Club in Boston.

"Oh," he said instantly, "it was *Red Fox* by Sir Charles George Roberts. I read it one summer when I was eight or nine years old, and it is what started my knowledge of nature that keeps turning up in my verse for children."

(Roberts was an accurate landscape painter and master of poetic structure who is considered the father of Canadian literature.)

Professor McCord has been retired from the Harvard faculty since 1962. He was approaching eighty-three when we talked.

What makes the difference doesn't have to be one of the classics, or "great" literature, or anything of the sort.

The difference can come even from comic books—when they help make it fun for you to learn to read.

Jim Jonard today manages a major automobile dealership in Westerville, Ohio. He's succeeded in a dozen different kinds of work, from teaching college chemistry to driving a coal truck.

The son of a coal miner, he had no allowance and precious few nickels as a boy, five going on six. And a nickel was what it cost then to buy a comic book, a *Superman*, or a *Batman and Robin*—or even a serious one about a famous American, George Washington, or better still, a famous inventor, such as Thomas Edison.

Young Jim "fell in love with the art of reading" by devouring comics. He'd go next door to play, find a pile of comics, bury himself in them, and never get outside to run around.

Sometimes, he'd do this even at home. His father would get furious calling and calling around the block for him to come to supper, but no answer. All the time, Jim would be reading in some corner right inside the house.

"I would get so engrossed, I literally didn't hear anything," he recalls. "It's still that way, reading is so special."

His father was injured in the coal mines when Jim was fourteen. The next year, even before he had a license, Jim was driving a coal truck he'd shoveled full and would shovel empty.

Books at home? There weren't any. His folks hadn't had the chance to finish high school. They didn't read themselves, and they didn't read to Jim.

"It was not what you would call a rich cultural atmosphere," he remembers.

The comics fanned his interest in all kinds of reading—the backs of cereal boxes, the dictionary, even school books. But those last spoiled him for classes.

"I would have all my books for the year read by the end of the first month, and after that, school would be a great big bore." By the seventh grade, he was sitting in the front row of study hall, so he could reach the encyclopedia volumes on the shelves nearby.

Inventors particularly fascinated him.

"People who could take one thing and make something new out of it, they're what I like to read about most. I just liked to learn how things were put together, even anatomy."

And even Japanese. In the fall of 1981, Jonard went back to college, to nearby Ohio State, to study that language, one of the world's most difficult.

"We buy our cars from the Japanese. I figure if you are in a business where you are talking to Japanese people, you shouldn't just make them learn your language. It's a good thing to learn theirs, too."

————

Virginia H. Mathews is vice president of the Shoe String Press in Hamden, Connecticut. Our question took her back many years.

"The book was in my childhood where the symbolism was strong, the imagery very strong. I was only eight years old when I read *The Princess and the Goblin* by George MacDonald, a children's favorite—one of those books never outgrown. The emotional response I gave that book became a sustaining base that is part of me.

"From it came the feeling that if someone loves you, you're always all right, and you always will be able to find your way through the dark and difficult situations."

An idea from a book can stay with you for a lifetime.

At age five, George Fleharty was keeping out of mischief by stacking books while his mother visited her librarian friend.

One book had a picture of a cabin high in the mountains and an old man and a little girl. He stopped to read it. "It all seemed so peaceful, the beauty of nature, the simple life," Fleharty remembers. "It gave me an early awareness that life had something more to it than the pursuit of material objectives. And it brought out the romanticist in me."

The book was about the love a grandfather and a granddaughter had for each other. It's been a children's favorite for nearly a century, and George Fleharty never forgot it.

As an adult, he was big in business. Eventually, he ran many different major corporations—a television station, a newspaper, two professional sports teams, two national park concessions, and an ice follies. He was mayor of Redding, California, for eight years, and directed thirteen political campaigns for his friend, California Governor Edmund "Pat" Brown.

But he paid a price.

"I became so involved and so obligated, it seemed I was running around in an airplane all the time. But it wasn't producing anything except more mortgages to the bank every year and keeping me too busy to get to know my family very well."

At age forty-six, after more than twenty years of scurrying, he did an about-face.

He gave up all his other businesses and kept only one—the Mt. McKinley National Park Lodge. To run it, he moved deep into the spectacular reaches of Alaska, where snow falls even in June and July, and for sixty miles and more you can see the granite peak that is the highest point in the United States.

Purposely, he built a simple life. The location was too remote for receiving television or even commercial radio. He subscribed to only one newspaper—the *International Herald Tribune*, printed in Paris. It arrived four or five days late, "but I didn't need to know the news right when it happened, anyway."

He felt better, younger, refreshed.

"Now I could go home at night and talk about what happened that day with my wife. Now I had time to read. Now I could go out for a walk up the trail and feel at peace with the world.

"Not many people in downtown Manhattan or other business centers would even know what I'm talking about. They'd think I was missing out on life. But I've had my fun and adventure, hobnobbing with the famous and the powerful, dealing in millions of dollars. I got lost there for a while, but eventually I came back to the simple life myself."

Now he and Mrs. Fleharty, all six children grown and away from home, live in their own log cabin by the side of the river and back in the woods.

He's there, of course, because of that idea that lasted a lifetime. "It all started with *Heidi*."

The Americanization of Edward Bok by Edward Bok, the autobiography of an editor of the *Ladies Home Journal*. For George McGhee, Washington, D.C., former United States ambassador to Turkey:

"I read this at age fourteen in Dallas when my family was having a hard time. It gave me confidence I could accomplish something."

When the novelist Paul Horgan was young, books started him toward his writing career.

When he was about nine: "*David Copperfield* by Dickens showed me that people in books could seem to be actual living creatures."

This was Dickens' most autobiographical novel in which the events that happen to David change him as a person.

And when he was about ten: "*The Count of Monte Cristo* by Dumas *père*, showed me how an extended story could sweep the reader along on an irresistible current of absorbing narrative."

It was the *Boy Scout Handbook*, the training manual for the Boy Scouts, for Raymond R. Kuhn.

He read it just before he was twelve, and it made him "want in." Then his troop had a visiting speaker, a sailor, a boatswain's mate.

"And, you know, I looked at that guy and said to myself, 'I'd like to be one of them.' "

Today Ray Kuhn is one of the most veteran sailors in all the navy. He is command master chief (the top-ranking enlisted man) in the submarine school the United States Navy runs in Groton, Connecticut. About five thousand new submariners go through every year to make it the largest sub school in the service.

Kuhn joined the navy in 1944. That's thirty-six-plus years, the last twenty-two of them in submarines. He's been at sea more than seventeen years.

His job is to advise the commanding officer on enlisted matters. He could have retired more than six years ago but really isn't giving the matter much thought.

"I guess I just like the navy. I live in a navy house, I work with some congenial people who know where they're going, and with some kids who don't know where they're going, and if I can help them, good. I talk with everyone from seamen to admirals, and I doubt it would be as fulfilling in retirement. Now I don't take the boat home with me at night, but by early morning, I'm rarin' to go again."

———

The Book of Wonders, an encyclopedia of natural and mechanical phenomena. For Richard Stoufer, Council Bluffs, Iowa, retired mechanical engineer who specialized in building elevators:

"I read it when I was five. It made me inquisitive about how machinery works and why. I stayed that way the rest of my life."

———

Barbara Bannon a slow reader?

The executive editor of *Publishers Weekly* in New York City, in charge of book reviewing for the publication for a dozen years, a slow reader?

Not now, but once...

"I was going to a progressive school, and when at eight years old I was the worst reader in class, it was suggested I needed remedial help.

"The family was appalled. My mother took me into a bookstore one day and asked me to pick out a book I thought I'd like to read. I picked a children's story and picture book about a family of cats. I can't give you the name, but I can still visualize it.

"We went home and spent an afternoon just sitting together, and somehow in talking with my mother and in reading this book I was really interested in, everything clicked in my head, and I went to school the next morning able to read, and I haven't stopped since."

Dan Lacy. Book people just about everywhere know this senior vice-president of McGraw Hill in New York City.

Raggedy Man by poet James Whitcomb Riley, he said.

"I learned to read on it.

"I started school late because I'd been ill, so I was six or more when I went. The first day I was there, the teacher wrote the word *see* on the board and explained how to sound out the letters and make the word.

"She gave us pencil and paper to write it out. I remember it was a short yellow pencil with a chewed end.

"And a great light came over me. It was the first time I had really realized that this was a code, and you could break it.

"So I came tearing home, and my parents had given me a copy of *Raggedy Man*, and I sat there with it, and they explained to me what the codes for the other letters were, and within a couple of weeks I could read it aloud with some fluency, and this struck me as the greatest miracle that ever happened in the world."

We are a mile and a half down inside the Grand Canyon. There is a small landing area where the mule train and its passengers rest on the way up from the floor of the canyon. A few short trees, a breathtaking view, but no facilities, no water.

Up the trail comes a party of one, a man hiking, not riding, yet breathing easily—scarcely any sweat. This is Paul Beach, at fifty-eight the sixth most senior pilot of the 750 flying for Hughes Airwest, putting into practice some of the taste for adventures he acquired as a youngster when he read a book of first-person experiences of some other adventurers.

"There were articles by Admiral Byrd about flying to the South Pole, and by the World War I flying ace Eddie Rickenbacker, and others, and I knew I wanted to be a flier from that moment on."

This was his first trip into the Grand Canyon. He and his wife and friends had stayed overnight at Phantom Ranch deep inside the canyon. They had come because "I fly over this beautiful country all the time, and it's always a challenge to see what it's like on the ground."

Captain Beach has logged some twenty-eight thousand hours in the air. After vacation, he'll again be in command of a multi-million-dollar jet to Salt Lake City to Seattle to Reno to Las Vegas, then back home to Phoenix.

Anyone who knows anyone in Michigan will tell you that the one person who knows more Michiganians than anyone else is Steve Nisbet. He has been a school teacher, superintendent, vice-president of the Gerber Baby Food company, co-chairman of a constitutional convention, and a member of many boards.

One of Steve Nisbet's ideas always has been that "to be successful and a contributor to solving our world problems you must also be an achiever and not a failure." And his inspiration for that comes from *The Story of the Man Who Didn't Know Much*, about a man who kept trying in the face of adversity, by W. A. Murray published in 1889.

"It taught me that nothing is too difficult if you believe in it, are willing to work and to overcome difficulties to address it."

(Steve, a widower, was particularly interested in our visit to him in Grand Rapids, Michigan because he knew Patricia and I had recently been married. He wanted to tell us about his own plans, for he'd tracked down a former sweetheart whom he found to be a widow, and they had set their own wedding date. Just like us—except that at the time, Steve was eighty-five and his bride, almost that.)

For Bill Veeck, former owner of the Chicago White Sox professional baseball team, the biggest difference has been "the greatest gift I've ever received—not just one book, because I read about 250 a year, but the pleasure of reading, which my daddy gave to me by reading to my sister and me when I was a young boy."

Veeck said, "I happen to believe in escape; it's something we all need." But then he pointed out an occupational hazard of a professional baseball team owner:

"Baseball to many people is an escape. But for me, I have to have an escape *from* baseball, and it's a book because with a book, you can be anything.

"On television, somebody else determines what you can be because they do the programming.

"But with the book and thousands of new titles printed a year, you can be anything you want.

"For example, take Sir Arthur Conan Doyle's books. Most people say, aha, *Sherlock Holmes* is the best. But no, I say *The White Company* was better because in it I could relive the Norman invasion of Brittany." *The White Company*, a historical novel, was Doyle's first.

_____

Don Lee Keith, New Orleans newspaper reporter and editorial writer, magazine editor, free-lancer:

"I grew up in Wheeler, Mississippi, population 217. Entertainment was what you might call limited, especially if you were a curious child, so I had learned to read by the time I went to school at age five. The first thing I learned when I got to school was that I wasn't supposed to know how to read, so I never paid any attention to that Dick and Jane and Sally stuff because they were boring. Anyway, by that time I had found something else that interested me: a book I found in the attic, *The Poems of Eugene Field*.

"That was the first time I realized that through the printed word, emotions could be elicited from an individual.

"In this book there were poems like 'Little Boy Blue,' which taught me that the printed word could elicit tears, and I squalled my eyes out every time I read it. I had to limit myself to only one time a week on it. And something called 'The Gingham Dog and the Calico Cat,' which taught me drama in the printed word. There was a poem called 'Seeing Things,' which taught me fear and loathing. And wonderful little 'Wynken, Blynken, and Nod.'

"It was at that time I became fascinated by the power of the printed word to evoke certain emotion in the reader. After that, I suppose I had no choice other than to become a writer. That doesn't mean I was precocious; that just means I was bored as hell growing up in Wheeler, Mississippi."

_____

Norman Cousins, longtime distinguished editor of *The Saturday Review* and now a member of the faculty of the University of California at Los Angeles, knew the answer at once:

"I have a very clear recollection of when I was twelve years old of *The Autobiography of Lincoln Steffens*," the life story of an American reporter, student of ethics and politics, a muckraker in his early twentieth century attempts to reform government.

"At that time, parents were giving that book to their children mostly because of the first part where the description of Steffens' childhood was very vivid. Even now I have an unforgettable picture of Steffens' first experience with his pony.

"But to me the most exciting part of the book was the description of his career as a muckraker, what happened when he got into journalism, how he got into the engineering of consent in terms of public issues, persuading people, especially in small towns.

"I can still see that town meeting in Greenwich, Connecticut, where he went to the blackboard and explained to the townspeople how their town, any small town, really works, and what had to be done if the town, in fact, was to be representative of the people's interest.

"That was when I decided to go into journalism."

———

They couldn't keep her mouth shut.

Doris Saunders began school at the James E. Carter Elementary, Fifty-eighth and Michigan, Chicago, and:

"I was a talker, and in those days, for that they put sticky tape on your mouth. In the first and second grade, they kept the stuff on my mouth all day long. It tasted horrible; it tasted like it was made out of somebody's glue."

Of course, she wasn't in the second grade very long.

"My teacher caught me reading *Camille* hiding inside my Elson's second reader. She took me to the principal's office, and I had to bring my mother to school.

"The principal wanted to know why I was reading that book, and I explained that I had finished the second reader the second day I got the book, so I didn't have anything to read, so I brought a book from home.

"She wanted to know what the book was about, so I told her it was about this lady who was sick and in love with this young man, and his father didn't like her, and she was dying, and they were in love. And she said:

" 'Well, out of the mouths of babes! Clearly we can't have her contaminating our other second graders who have to stay with Elson's second reader, so let's see how she does in the third grade.' "

"So they jumped me one whole year and later jumped me twice more. I missed some kinds of mathematics. I still don't know square root very well, and I had to learn fractions on my own. But the greater challenge of advancing grades kept me interested—and kept my mouth shut more."

Mrs. Saunders spent many years on *Ebony* magazine and now is a professor of journalism at Jackson State University, Jackson, Mississippi. Camille, she said, was her mother's middle name, and she has named her own daughter Ann Camille.

———

Anne Bernays, born in New York City, educated at Wellesley and Barnard, worked in publishing, married, started to write, published six novels, brought up three daughters. Now she teaches at Emerson College as writer-in-residence.

"I started to write at the age of twenty-seven when my first daughter was just born, and I turned out an enormous number of words. I've been writing even since because this is the way I respond to my experience, and this is the way of bringing some kind of order out of what I see, of making some kind of response to it. I automatically write it down."

Her book is *The Forsyte Saga* by John Galsworthy, a history of a typical solid and substantial English family. She explained:

"Part of the difference a book makes to you is at what point in your life you read it. It just happened that I read this book when my psychological needs were for just it.

"It was the first time I realized that my parents had an emotional life entirely separately from mine. It opened up the world to me in the strangest way. It was like people finding God. Until that moment, I was overly dependent on my parents, but after it, I moved off into my own life. It allowed me to mature in a way I don't think any shrink could have done. I don't think anything else could have done.

"It was just magic."

Barbara Tuchman wins prizes for her marvelously interesting and meticulously researched historical books. She began down that trail when very young.

"In fact I was only six. Living at home in New York City, I read three books written for primary school children, and they started my fascination with history, and I've been at it ever since."

They were *The Scottish Chiefs* by Jane Porter, whose historical fiction preceded the novels of Sir Walter Scott; *The White Company* by Sir Arthur Conan Doyle, and *The Belgian Twins* by Lucy Fitch Perkins, based on the experience of Belgian children who find a haven in New York during World War I.

Memories are made in childhood. And Helen Bradley recalls an Emilie Loring book:

"I don't know the name of it, but there was this quotation, the heroine was quite taken with it: 'Give to the world the best you have, and the best will come back to you.'

"I was about fourteen at the time, and I adopted this as my motto, plus 'if something is worth doing, it's worth doing well.' "

When we talked, she was finishing library school at the University of South Florida and working in the language and literature division of the Tampa Public Library.

The Wizard of Oz by Frank Baum, details the adventures of Dorothy in the land of the Munchkins as she travels with the Scarecrow, the Tin Woodsman, the Cowardly Lion and all. For Dr. W. Eugene Mayberry, chairman of the board of governors, Mayo Clinic, Rochester, Minnesota:

"At the age of nine, I was enthralled with the entertainment of it and with the joy of discovering that one could be so entertained by reading."

THE WONDERFUL WORLD OF WORDS

Sometimes the conversations we had, even with first-met strangers, became very personal, even intimate. Right away, we were discussing love affairs our interviewees had been having, not infrequently for most of their lives.

That was all right, though, because the object of the affection turned out to be books about words, the wonderful world of words, and we shared those feelings. Such fascination there can be, such endless variety and surprise. Such satisfaction from achieving the precise fit of word to thought or deed. Bob Cromie was an example.

"Book Beat" was his program on public television, and the book beat is what Cromie covered for many years for the *Chicago Tribune*, and still does when he brings authors to discuss their books on Chicago's WGN.

He's now retired from the *Tribune*, where for thirty-eight years he was reporter, rewrite man, war correspondent, and sportswriter before becoming book editor and columnist.

In addition to being a book man, Cromie is a word man.

"I really like the dictionary. Obviously, it's a key. If you're reading something and don't know about the dictionary or aren't using it, you'll stumble through and wonder what the author meant. In most cases, the dictionary can help you.

"When I was young, I used to make lists of words, sort of romantic words, words like *forlorn*, and *dawn*, and *dusk*, and that sort of thing. It was a big help and probably one of the reasons I became a newspaperman, I had this early love affair with words.

"Beyond that, the poets. Shakespeare, for example. 'The sun, a fair hot wench in flame-colored taffeta.' Oh, what a master. Shows you what can be done with ordinary words.

"Or Rupert Brooke. 'If I should die, think only this of me, that there's some corner of a foreign field that is forever England.' That gives me a chill.

"I love the sound and the way words convolute themselves, but I also like to find someone using a word in an unusual manner. Keats, for example, in 'The Eve of St. Agnes,' speaks of the 'silver snarling trumpets.' What a marvelous way to describe trumpets. They *are* harsh. And they sneer at you, more or less. But who but Keats? I don't think anyone had ever done that, that well before."

Even in an interview, Bob Cromie remains a reviewer.

"By the way, have you ever heard of an author named Peter Beagle? He's marvelous.

"His first novel came out when he was nineteen, maybe twenty-one but I think nineteen. He wrote *A Fine and Private Place* about a man who lived in a mausoleum in Central Park and was fed by ravens. He wrote *The Last Unicorn*—a unicorn is searching with the aid of a magician and various medieval types to see if there are any unicorns left, if he's the last one. And he has a new book out called *The Fantasy Worlds of Peter Beagle*, with some beautiful short stories, including 'Come, Lady Death.'

"He is a true wordsmith."

———

Virginia Burnside in Seattle told us of a similar love affair. She is a member of the Seattle Library Board, a professor of journalism at Seattle University, a newspaper columnist, and a promoter of Webster's *Unabridged Dictionary*.

"I happen to be a lover of words. I'm a lover of information. I'm a lover of precise thought. And there's no way you can know words or think precisely without knowing the dictionary.

"When I was thirteen, I read the dictionary completely through. I outlined what I had read. I absorbed and remembered what I had read.

"It made a profound influence on my life. It directed the course I would take in college. It contributed materially to the scholastic achievements that I obtained. It has been my companion, my delight, and my joy.

"For the remainder of my life, and I presume until the day that I die, I will love words, and I will love precise thought. The two are inextricably related.

"You can't think clearly, you can't think precisely without knowing words.

"So that's why I say, 'Webster's, I love you!' "

———

The dictionary meant more than words to Crawford Lincoln. It also paid his salary.

Lincoln, now president of the Old Sturbridge Village Association in Massachusetts, for twenty-five years was secretary and vice-president and once even acting president of the G.&C. Merriam Company, publishers of *Webster's New Collegiate Dictionary*.

"This was the volume that saw me through the years of academic study and gave me a feel for the way language operates. Coming to Merriam and working with the book, I began to see how language is very definitely an instrument of the people who use it. The dictionary is a de-scriptive rather than a pre-scriptive approach. I found an understanding of its richness, its growth, its change over the years, and its infinite variety.

"The dictionary made me more conscious of ideas in the world around me, and sharpened my awareness of them and my ability to deal with concepts other than those I had grown up with."

———

Edwin Newman, star NBC news correspondent since 1952, is comforting to meet. In his office, he looks and sounds much the way he looks and sounds on the air.

A twinkle in both the voice and the eye (there was a time his goal was to become a humorous writer). A *bon mot* waiting to happen. Almost never has to search for the right word.

His *Strictly Speaking* and *A Civil Tongue*, which are both appeals to use the English language more precisely, have had great receptions. He didn't do it single-handedly, he points out, but: "You even have banks and insurance companies advertising that their contracts can be read and understood. Some plain language laws here and there. Ridicule directed at pomposity to a degree I have never known before.

"Attempts to reform government language, the language of the income tax return, for example. Also a requirement now in some colleges and universities that freshmen take courses in English so that they'll be able to write a simple sentence.

"So clearly something is happening. Whether enough to reverse the trend, I don't know. I doubt it. There are such tremendous forces that make for the deterioration of the language."

The book that made the greatest difference to him? Newman remembers that when he was an undergraduate at the University of Wisconsin, "I became tremendously interested in the works of Thorstein Veblen.

"I read *The Theory of the Leisure Class*, read his books on imperial Germany and the industrial revolution, his theories about the instinct of workmanship, his theories about business management, and the theory of conspicuous consumption, a brilliant, marvelous idea.

"The phrase that has stayed with me more than any other that Veblen used is 'the instinct of workmanship.'

"Why does someone work well and somebody else not work well? The answer is 'the instinct of workmanship.'

"I've always felt that when when you're writing, you're writing for yourself. You may begin by wanting to write good copy so that the editor won't throw it back to you, but at some point, the instinct of workmanship takes over. It takes over, and I've always been that way."

The dictionary, any dictionary, is the choice for Mrs. Bessie Moore, Little Rock, Arkansas, vice-chairman of the National Commission on Libraries and Information Science, and executive director of the Arkansas State Council on Economic Awareness.

"It made me a person with better understanding of people and events. I wouldn't have the richness of life I've had if I hadn't learned early on the richness of the language."

He never went to college but James Russell Wiggins was well-educated enough to become editor of the *Washington Post* because of his early love for words and reading. He was introduced to his book in high school in Luverne, Minnesota—*Twelve Centuries of English Poetry and Prose*, edited by Newcomer and Andrews.

"It gave me the idea of the importance of literature in communication. Our language is really a language of metaphor, and if you took out everything metaphoric between the covers of this book, or if you took it out of Shakespeare, you would have to spend paragraphs and pages saying what you could in a phrase with metaphors.

"Communication is by no means limited to the mastery of grammar and a vocabulary. Ordinary speech includes an incredible array of figures, likenesses without which civilized people really cannot communicate."

You use your interest in good literature every day of your life, Wiggins points out.

"What you stuff into your mind, it's like the computer. The input governs the output. If you're not widely read and continuously widely read, you're diminished in your ability to communicate your own ideas and your ability to grasp new ones."

In 1969, Wiggins realized the dream of so many big city newspaper types. He bought a small weekly in Ellsworth, Maine. In a decade he tripled its circulation, helping prove that words well used attract audiences everywhere.

———

When you interview Studs Terkel, you miss a bet if you don't ask him about his own great interviewing ability.

"I don't know that I'm great. I'd say I'm a good interviewer because I'm a carpenter who carries his tool chest with him. That's all.

"A good carpenter is a good craftsman. Notice how I've marked this book in preparation for an interview with the author? I have to do that, you see, so now these are things we'll talk about. So this is my tool chest—I read the book.

"Why shouldn't everybody do it? Do you say to a carpenter who walks in with his tool chest, 'Oh, you've brought your tool chest? My God, you brought your saw. Isn't that marvelous?'

"Interviewing is listening. If your interviewee knows you're listening, that's half the battle. You're really interested, you're not just a guy from Mount Olympus, from ABC or NBC.

" 'What do you think of busing?' That doesn't mean anything. Or 'What do you think of ERA?' That's not important. Well, it is, but you want to know *why* that person feels. What made the person say what he said? Then you go back to the beginnings; you got to go back to the life of that person, the dream of that person, or the fear of that person.

"That's my equipment, and of course the big one: Curiosity, curiosity."

His book? The Chicago author and radio personality said *Adventures of Huckleberry Finn* by Mark Twain (Samuel Clemens), in which Huck runs away from Miss Watson, the Widow Douglas, and his brutal father to found a family with the Negro slave Jim.

The book taught him, "in the words of Martin Luther King, that there is something beyond the written law; there is the law of human decency."

———

"Try selling hot dogs instead," George Bernard Shaw told him. William Chase had become a Shaw fan when he bought for forty-five cents a little pamphlet, *The Author's Apology from "Mrs. Warren's Profession,"* a Shaw play about organized prostitution. In his enthusiasm, he wrote the English playwright, "I'm starting a book shop dealing just in Shaviana; may we use your name?"

Shaw's reply came in red ink on a corner of the letter:

"You cannot run a book shop on the work of a single author, especially one whose name repels so many customers. You are evidently not a born bookseller; try selling hot dogs."

That sank the book shop idea, but Chase later established a Shaw Society of America, through which he got Shaw to release his ninety-fourth (and last) birthday anniversary message.

Chase founded the Apple Tree Press to publish Shaw's last will. Eventually he found time from his work as librarian for the Flint, Michigan, *Journal* to create *Chase's Calendar of Annual Events*, a reference source no library would want to be caught without.

———

For some authors, their own books made the greatest difference. Here are reports from four:

It was his own first novel, *This Fortress World*, a work of science fiction, for James Gunn, a writer with nearly three million copies of twenty-five books in print. Now a professor at the University of Kansas, he said, "It proved I could write a novel and have it published. It strengthened the notion that I could make it in this field."

———

In the City Lights bookstore of San Francisco, we went up eleven narrow, steep stairs ("good thing the fire inspector hasn't been here for twenty-five years") to a makeshift mezzanine office. There the proprietor, Lawrence Ferlinghetti, with the bluest blue eyes you ever did see, held forth.

"The most important book in my life was my own first book published in New York by New Directions. It was called *A Coney Island of the Mind*, and it has sold almost a million copies.

"The difference it made was it allowed me to live as a poet should live, not having to work in soul-killing offices like the Bank of America or some other place like that."

(*A Coney Island of the Mind* is a selection of poems mirroring the attitude of the beat generation toward the time—1959.)

Jade Snow Wong was brought up in a basement in Chinatown. When she was twenty-six, she wrote *Fifth Chinese Daughter*, the story of an American girl of Chinese parentage who grew up in San Francisco. She was the first American-Chinese woman to write that kind of story, she told us at her desk in the back of her San Francisco Chinese boutique:

"I did not expect it to make much of an impact on my life or the lives of other people, but it sold more than a quarter of a million copies and has been translated into other languages all over the world.

"It made a difference in my life by bringing many people to me, by mail or in person. They come here from all over the world bringing their experiences, and what I did not foresee was their finding in my book an experience similar to their own lives.

"The story I told was that of myself as a repressed female. The real story of the book that appeals to people is that out of repression, you can find individuality in America."

Orientals did not believe her book could have happened, the author said. They thought the Voice of America had invented it for propaganda. So the United States State Department sent her to China to speak, and "that brought me personally into other areas of the world and made me an international citizen."

The author of *The Lilies of the Field*:

"I wrote it in odd times and didn't make it a major project. While it was still longhand, I read it to Bunny and said, 'What could I do with it?' and she said she couldn't think of anything. I couldn't either. I couldn't imagine anyone publishing a book about a black man and a group of nuns. It had all the taboos.

"So I just put it away and didn't even type it. Several months later, Doubleday wanted to make an anthology. I didn't feel like collecting the things, so I suggested they might like to start with a brand new thing I wrote. Within a week, four people there were enthused about it, and boy, we wrapped it up.

"I never was more surprised in my life."

But *Lilies* was not the book that made the greatest difference to William E. Barrett. That one came earlier, written over four years at night "in a cubbyhole on the scholars desk in the Library of Congress, after I'd turned out articles and short stories and detectives all day to earn a living."

The big one was his first novel, *Woman on Horseback*, a biography of Francisco Lopez, dictator of Paraguay in the 1860s and 1870s and of his mistress Eliza Lynch. "It didn't make much money, but it did establish me as someone who could write books, and I never quite got away from them."

Part of Barrett's writing technique:

"I gave each character a name and also a twelfth birthday observance.

"I have to know each person and in a formative stage. The twelfth birthday just struck me as being a time when somebody is shaping. He's neither one thing or another. When I know a person when he's twelve years old and still dominated by adults, and he's got his own mind reaching out for things, it's a very good time. I know his comrades, the people he plays with, his adults, his parents, all the casuals that come into his life.

"It makes me feel I know the character before I start to write a book about him. Others seem to just pull them out of the air, and you can't do that."

Part of his philosophy:

"A novelist should write of life as he sees it. No matter how odd his view on the world may seem to others, he will probably find readers, perhaps many, who see life as he sees it. A novelist, after all, is neither prophet nor priest, nor is he merely an entertainer. He is a reporter of lives of people, real or imaginary."

Bill and Bunny Barrett were married in 1925. They were very much still in love when we talked with them in their Denver apartment, fifty-five years later.

———————

Jane Gordon is the director of the Louisa M. Alcott house museum in Lexington, Massachusetts. Between two church meetings one Sunday, she talked to us while sitting at the handmade writing desk by the front window of the upstairs bedroom. Here Miss Alcott wrote *Little Women*, the adventures of the March family, set in a small mid-nineteenth century New England town.

"Louisa was the kind of person who prized her quiet time, who liked to come up to this room and be alone and do her writing. She wrote in fits and starts, sometimes for several hours at a time. Other days she couldn't write at all.

"She wrote a lot of stories with fairy tale characters, a lot of what we'd call today Gothic thriller stories. During the Civil War, she was a nurse with a Union army hospital in Washington, D.C., and from then on, she more and more based her books on incidents and characters she'd really known.

"When in 1868 her publisher asked her to write a book for girls, she decided to base her novel, *Little Women*, on the episodes and experiences of her own family. The characters are the actual four Alcott girls, and most of the book is very close to the truth. Louisa felt that if there were an interest in this book, it would be because the girls were so true to real life, and their experiences were not so glamorous, but they were someone other girls could relate and identify with and feel could have been their own family.

"Her father was a very different kind of schoolteacher from most in his day. He felt it was very important for children to learn about themselves before they started studying the universe around them. He felt one of the most important things children could learn was to converse with other people, so he generated many discussions. He also taught the children to write by having them keep journals, which they did all their lives. He started out the journal for each of them when she was an infant, making the entries, recording every development. Then they carried on throughout their lives. When Louisa was writing *Little Women*, she could turn back to the pages in the journals, either literally or by discussing the book with her sisters, and use that material for the book.

"Louisa never married. She decided to remain a free spinster and paddle her own canoe. She said that her pen was her husband and her books were her children."

Mrs. Gordon's book is, you'll not be surprised, *Little Women*.

"Those were experiences I could see myself having. Jo, Louisa herself, is a very willful girl, very much a tomboy, hates to have to dress up like a lady, hates to act properly, and certainly that's what I was feeling as a young girl. I didn't want to have to do things just the way everyone else did. *Little Women* was reinforcement for me, gave me the encouragement to go on."

SOMEONE I'D LIKE TO BE LIKE

He'd dropped out of school in the eighth grade, and money from his jobs went toward family expenses. When he was fourteen, he read a biography of General John J. Pershing, commander-in-chief of United States forces in Europe during World War I. And as soon as he could (in fact, a bit sooner, for he fibbed about his age) he enlisted in the army and eventually himself became a general officer.

This was James M. Gavin, one of the leaders of the American forces in World War II, then ambassador to France, and president and chairman of Arthur D. Little, Inc.

He's forgotten both title and author of the book, but not its influence.

"That's why I ended up at West Point. I wanted to be like General Pershing."

———

Book heroes and heroines, both real-life and captured from an author's fantasy, made a big difference in lives of many others.

Sometimes they chose the same career as the model in the book. Sometimes they tried to emulate the personality of the idol.

And some simply recognized that they were like their book person and were headed in the right direction.

———

Clarence Darrow for the Defense by Irving Stone, the biography of Darrow's career at the bar and backgrounds of his famous cases, was an inspiration for Frank Mankiewicz, Washington, D.C., now president of National Public Radio. Earlier, he was an executive in the Peace Corps, wrote a syndicated Washington column, anchored a television newscast, served as press secretary to Senator Robert Kennedy, and directed the presidential campaign of George McGovern:

"It made me realize that people who fought that kind of battle could win now and then and could make a difference. I resolved that I could be such a person, and I've tried."

———

Leaves of Grass by Walt Whitman, is the collection of poems. The longest is "Song of Myself," describing the joyful experiences of the poet. For Stanley Idzerda, former president and now professor, College of St. Benedict's, St. Joseph, Minnesota, and for four years in charge of processing the collected papers of the Marquis de Lafayette at Cornell University:

"The difference that made was in the way I feel about myself and what I think it means to live on this continent where everything is possible and expansiveness never ends. 'I saw in Louisiana a live oak growing. All alone it stood there, joyously uttering leaves of darkness.' That's what I want to be as a human being, the kind of role model I want to be for the students."

———

Pride and Prejudice by Jane Austen, a gentle satire of English country life in the early nineteenth century. For Mickey Friedman, who covers books and authors for the San Francisco Examiner:

"It gave me a role model, a wonderfully witty heroine, very self-sufficient, very independent. I wanted to be like that heroine. I'm still trying."

Florence Ladd, psychologist and dean of students at Wellesley College, Wellesley, Massachusetts, thought she was looking in a mirror.

Her book, *An Anthropologist at Work*: Writings of Ruth Benedict, edited by Margaret Mead, describing how one anthropologist goes about her work, her emotional life expressed in her poetry, and her contributions to her discipline.

"I never met her, but I feel I know her. There are so many parallels between her life and mine—parallels in quality of marriage, parallels in becoming a social scientist. She also was a poet, which is a part of me I value and treat in a private way, just as her poetry was private.

"She was my model, my pattern. I resemble Ruth Benedict. She became a psychological point of reference for me."

The Autobiography of Benjamin Franklin, one of the "fathers" of the United States, much of whose philosophy is relevant to the twentieth century, was named by two.

For Gunther Barth, professor of history, University of California-Berkeley, and immigrant to the United States from Germany when he was a youth in the 1950s:

"It had that mixture of an enormous degree of humanitarian concern combined with a shrewd defense of self-interest. I had never met that happy mixture before, but it's one I have tried to emulate."

And for Ralph Reeder, professor emeritus of agricultural information, Purdue University, West Lafayette, Indiana:

"In difficult times, that book helped me keep on an even keel. It kept me on the side of common sense and good humor, since he had both qualities. Of course, so far as making me a statesman to France, I didn't do very well on that."

Abraham Lincoln was six feet four inches tall, and Frank Cucksey doesn't quite reach four feet six inches. Never mind, Lincoln was Cucksey's "favorite hero."

"I fell in love with him years and years ago. Wherever I could, I tried to live my life like him."

Cucksey was in show business twenty years. When the Munchkins danced along with Judy Garland in *The Wizard of Oz*, he was the one who stepped out and handed her a bouquet of flowers.

He's now retired from work as a security guard at the Ringling Museum in Sarasota, Florida, so he has more time to read "anything about Abraham Lincoln."

The author of *Books that Changed the World* (a million copies sold in fourteen languages) and *Books that Changed America* himself was most influenced by the books written by Horatio Alger, Jr.

Robert D. Downs, seventy-seven years old, retired librarian at the University of Illinois, Urbana, Illinois, comments that "those books are considered trash by many people, but on the other hand, they influenced a great many American boys in the late nineteenth, early twentieth centuries.

"They showed me that a boy who grew up in a family of very modest means, very limited income (which described our family very well), by working hard, by being honest and industrious, by associating with the right people, could achieve success.

"They were an inspiration to me. After all, I was just a country boy and with very little experience with the world. If I hadn't read, I wouldn't have gone on to advanced education; I would have ended as a farm laborer."

Markings by Dag Hammarskjöld, a diary of the Swedish statesman's debate between "his cravings as a human animal" and his "longing for the cross" resolved in his identification with God.

For Ivar Nelson, book publisher and seller in Moscow, Idaho:

"He was very committed to the proposition that people owe a debt to society, that life is a combination of your relationship to yourself and to society. I decided to follow that too. I was in the American foreign service as part of the delegation to the United Nations, and I was in the Peace Corps before that."

Marvin Jensen, Cedar Falls, Iowa, professor of communications at Northern Iowa University, made the same choice of a book that made the difference:

"Hammarskjöld showed me that the consequence of standing for something may be loneliness—but that kind of loneliness is endurable."

Westerns—any westerns. For William Carey Graves, fire captain in Grapevine, Texas:

"The heroes were always doing good deeds for others. They made me want to do the same thing, which is why I'm in the fire department."

Happy Trails, by Roy Rogers, the story of Rogers and Dale Evans. For Lonnie Tilley, Mountain Home, Arkansas, pilot of the Arkansas Department of Highways ferry that carries U.S. 62 traffic across Norfolk Lake east of Mountain Home:

"I learned about their Christian way of life and tried to raise my family the way they did."

"I was very much a typical high-school girl, very much a failure because I didn't have a date on Saturday night. And most of my concern was where the next beer was coming from or whether I had Spalding saddle shoes, and gosh, isn't it too bad that I've got pimples, and how awful that I'm too big to be a cheerleader, and you feel, just totally you feel like you're a real big nothing.

"Another concern and worry I had at that time: What if someone doesn't ask me to marry him? And then what will I do? But if someone ever does ask me out, what will I talk about?

"I was really into that kind of thing, and then I had to read a book for a book report, and I don't even know where I got a book about Margaret Sanger because I'm sure the school library didn't have it, and the public library didn't have it.

"It wasn't well written, but it described a woman who knew what she believed in. And what she believed in—birth control—in the days before it even was talked about out loud, was indeed very unpopular.

"She risked almost everything in her personal life to accomplish an end, and she struck me as the kind of woman I wanted to be. Out of that book, several years later, I got very active in family planning. I was in Illinois when it was still illegal to give out birth control information, and I worked for the Board of Health and was fired as a test case because I kept referring people to Planned Parenthood.

"She was a woman of great courage and made me feel that morals were a relative thing and that under no circumstances can or should we force our own moral judgments on other people.

"Also she made me realize that it didn't really matter that I didn't have a date on Saturday night, that women could do something else."

(Nancy Gray does indeed do something else. She's mayor of Fort Collins, Colorado and wife of a Colorado State University professor.)

SOME PERSONAL CHOICES

All the interviews were good but at the end of any day, it was possible to look back and say that this one or that one had had a particular impact. Sometimes that was because of who said it, or what was said, or where and under what circumstances it was said.

The "Book Ends" editor of the *New York Times Book Review*, for instance, wouldn't name just one book but went down a different path:

"The right to have a library card on which I could borrow three or four books a week from my local branch in Brooklyn made the greatest difference in my life," Herbert Mitgang said. "That enabled me to read anything without charge, and I was proud to be able to take books out and to be trusted, to carry them openly and proudly in the streets."

———

A comment from Jade Snow Wong comes to mind.

"For someone like me growing up knowing only Chinese—we didn't speak English at home—the ability to go to a library and get unrestricted books, just the whole experience of reading free, is the greatest thing for ethnic groups growing up in America.

"I was in China in 1972 and again in 1979 and in a socialist state like that where people's thoughts are being manipulated, they are not free to read what they please.

"Anyone going to the Peking library has to write down what books he wants to read, and that request is reviewed by some committee. They always have a record of what somebody has read.

"That's a very precious freedom, the liberty we have here that most people take for granted."

———

A woman who helped her husband drive a truck was memorable. For Elizabeth Yon, Chesapeake, Virginia, it was the *Encyclopedia Americana*, which she'd bought from a door-to-door salesman more than twenty years before.

"That gave me lots of information, and also I found out how to research it, how to use it. Also how to fix my car, a lot about heraldry, and how to make pickles."

What she didn't report the first time we talked was that from the encyclopedia she had learned about treatments for illness in her family and through that, had discovered her mother was taking conflicting medicines. "She probably saved her mother's life," her doctor said.

———

Her book helped a North Carolina wife to have better fights with her husband.

It is *The Intimate Enemy: How to Fight Fair in Love and Marriage* by George Robert Bach and Peter Wyden.

"The arguments my husband and I had from time to time had left me feeling frustrated, so I decided to apply some of the suggestions the book made the next time an argument developed," said Jacqueline Kirkman, of Charlotte.

"We now feel that any argument we have can be constructive rather than destructive."

———

Ziolkowski is the name. Ziolkowski. A crazy man carving up a whole mountain.

Crazy Horse Mountain in South Dakota. *Reader's Digest* calls it one of the seven wonders of the modern world.

A monument to the Indian chief who beat up General Custer at Little Big Horn. A whole mountain turned into a giant god-size sculpture of the chief astride his horse. Nearly seven million tons of granite blasted away, with the figures just now taking shape.

And the artist, not a crazy man at all but surely one of the world's most ambitious storytellers in stone, has worked on this from his own middle age to old age, through broken bones and spinal operations and heart attacks.

If you hurry, you still can meet Korczak Ziolkowski, now in his seventies but still going strong. He has refused a $10 million federal subsidy for his work, so you'll have to pay $5 a carload to visit the Indian Museum of North America, inspect his sixty-one room log cabin studio home, take pictures of the mountain, see the twenty-foot-high scale model of the carving Korczak expects he won't live to finish.

The location is on Highways 16 and 385 between Hill City and Custer, South Dakota. Hours are dawn to dusk, year round.

The book for this man with the massive dream is *A History of*

Ancient Greek Literature by Gilbert Murray, a great scholar of the late 1800s.

"I carried it with me in a knapsack all during World War II. It went with me through mud, water, and blood.

"It was my intellectual beginning. It introduced me to the ancients and the foundation they laid for better history. It taught me we're living not just this moment, but the culmination of all the moments before this one, all those thousands of years.

"The lessons of the ancients taught me how to be able to work for tomorrow, a very distant tomorrow I won't be around to see."

Judge Woodrow Seals of the U.S. District Court in Houston, Texas read his statement to our tape recorder from the back seat of a car as we were driving to lunch. *The Boy Scout Handbook* was his choice:

" 'Be Prepared' is the motto of the Boy Scouts, and it became my guiding principle. I know a lot of great people to whom opportunity never came, but you ought to be prepared because you never know what hour on the stage the star is going to fall, and you have to be prepared to walk out on that stage and take that place."

It was no coincidence that we were on Sanibel Beach on the Gulf of Mexico west of Ft. Myers, Florida, one of the great shelling beaches of the world. We had planned this visit but not the coincidence that followed.

Patricia had the camera trained, and I was in my bathing trunks wading toward shellers digging industriously at six one Sunday morning. The tape recorder was catching the rumble of the surf and the cries of the seagulls as they circled.

Ann Dennis, a Jackson, Mississippi, real estate salesperson, and her husband were scratching shells from the sand. I approached, asked my question, and without any prompting, she named the Richard Bach book—*Jonathan Livingston Seagull*. The book is a parable about a seagull who loves to fly to test himself while other gulls merely search for food. The message is: there are no limits— the power of positive thinking.

In Boston, I wanted to go to the Navy Yard and see "Old Ironsides," the *Constitution*, that noble frigate that outfought everyone from the Barbary Coast pirates to the British Fleet in 1812 to establish a United States place on the seas.

It's not that I'm a sailing nut. Rather, I had remembered when as a child I'd taken some pennies to my second grade teacher to turn in for the schoolchildren's fund drive to restore this ship.

A crew of thirty-eight now keeps the *Constitution* in shape so hundreds of thousands of visitors can walk her gangplank every year.

Some of the crew were wearing the uniform of the U.S. sailors of the late eighteenth century. One of these was a tall young man named Leonard Quintavalla, a seaman apprentice on his first assignment after boot camp. His home is only fifteen minutes away in Saugus, but he'd never seen the *Constitution* before he was assigned to her. Now he's one of her proudest men as he explains her history and strikes the half hours on the ship's bell.

His book is *Sherlock Holmes* by Sir Arthur Conan Doyle, the adventures of the grand old detective who cleverly solves case after case.

"He was a very smart man, always one step ahead of everybody else, and that's how I try to pace myself."

Women are different—but that doesn't make them wrong, the first woman appointed assistant commissioner of education in Colorado told us.

Anna Marie Falsone's book is *The Managerial Woman* by Hennig and Jardim, an analysis of why women have trouble making it in management; it includes a study of twenty-five successful women managers.

"That book came out about the same time I was appointed assistant commissioner, and two of my friends seemed to think I needed it.

"I've now recommended it to a number of men who have sincerely told me they are interested in promoting women within their organization, but they really don't understand what I mean when I say, 'But women think differently. Women look at things differently. Our culture has raised women differently, so you shouldn't expect your women executives to approach a problem from the same perspective a man does.'

"It made it easier for me to realize that although I was often the only woman in a group and tended to analyze a situation differently from others did not mean that my approach was wrong."

Is the best-read person in all of Chicago a waiter at Riccardo's restaurant who once dug beets for a living?

If he isn't, then Bobbie Estrada must be close. His report of what he has read was one of the most extraordinary ones we received, and here it is:

"I was born in Mexico and all the formal schooling I had was there. Our family came to live in the United States in 1924, when I was thirteen. I learned the language in six months, then went out to buy magazines—the *Saturday Evening Post, Review of Reviews, Mentor, National Geographic*—and read, read, read.

"In 1930, I discovered the Chicago Public Library, and I've been going to it nearly every day for the past fifty years. I work at the restaurant both lunch and dinner, a split shift, so I have between two and five in the afternoon to go there and read everything from *A* to *Z*, from *atoms* to *zymosis*.

"I learned languages, I learned Greek and Arabic and German. I learned a lot of things, all from the library. I read the classics and the non-classics, everything.

"No matter how much you read, it's like in a forest, you can see only so many trees, you cannot cover everything."

His book? *Don Quixote*, by Cervantes, the adventures of an idealistic reformer who tries to right the injustices of the world.

"It broadened my outlook because it has so much wisdom. It put more light into my life. Before, I had a twenty-five-watt bulb and after reading it, I had a two-hundred-watt bulb in my life."

But he didn't stop with *Don Quixote*.

Then *War and Peace*, by Tolstoi, considered the greatest novel of novels, about Napoleon's invasion of Russia and retreat from Moscow.

And *Les Misérables*, by Victor Hugo, a novel of social consciousness in which the hero, Jean Valjean, is sentenced to prison for stealing a loaf of bread.

"Montaigne, of course. And William Shakespeare, he's a must.

"They all made my life greater. I became a better man, a better father, a better friend. I became a better everything else because of them for the rest of my life."

What would he still like to do, still like to read?

"Well, I'm a linguist. I like to learn languages. I'd like to learn Chinese, also to improve my Arabic.

"I'd also like to learn the Egyptian hieroglyphics so I could read The Book of the Dead in the original." (The Book of the Dead contains the wisdom and religion of the ancient Egyptians.)

Finally, a book that made a difference—but of a different kind.

His book made a great negative difference, according to Philip Sangiorgio, of San Diego, California.

"It was in a Roman history class my sophomore year in college when I read Livy's *The War with Hannibal*, a detailed account of that conflict. It made me decide to major in ancient history with the idea of becoming a professor. I'd passed my exams for the Ph.D., even took much of my dissertation research, when my wife became pregnant and I had to get a job.

"To my horror, I discovered the 'real world' cared little for 'all but dissertation' Ph.D.'s—I might have been well educated, but I was supremely unqualified and inexperienced for a 'real' job."

"Were it not for Livy, I might have majored in something useful, but I am only a postal clerk, shunned by former friends and associates as an embarrassment, and despised by all when their *TV Guide*s are late."

THERE ISN'T ANY ONE BEST

After a whole year of this, our conclusions are simple, and, perhaps, obvious:

1. Do books make a difference? You bet your life they do. Not to everyone, of course, for in no society in the world has a majority of the population ever been regular readers. But in the United States today more persons reported reading at least one book in the preceding six months than did so back before the start of nationwide television, by a margin of something like 55 to 33 per cent. The number of titles published and the sale of books and the dollars we spend for books—all these figures have gone up dramatically since the early 1950s.

2. Such a wide range of books Americans are interested in! Alcoholics Anonymous to the *Boy Scout Handbook*, *Don Quixote* to *The Sensuous Woman*. You cannot say there is anything like a single "national" book for Americans.

3. The reading experience is personal. So personal it borders on the intimate. One person writes, another reads. The communication link is joined. Something takes place between sender and receiver. It may or may not be what the author intended. It may or may not be what other readers feel. No matter; the impact is individual. And in a time when identity increasingly is lost, even drowned,

the reading of books may remain as one of the few truly personal acts left to us.

4. The purpose, the result of reading, also is personal. What may inform one may inspire another. The opening of a new career for one, reinforcement of an existing way of life for another. It depends upon what is going on inside the reader, it depends upon what that person's reading needs are the moment eye meets page.

5. In some cases—the Bible, for one—there can be different differences to different persons from the same book. Just another expression of the personal-ness.

6. Most of the books that made the most difference to a majority of the people we listened to would be classified as "literature" —but never appeared on a best-seller list.

7. There is no age when reading is most important. It always is important. Many a first book made the biggest difference, but so did others read during maturity.

8. What makes the difference, and what the difference is or will be, is not predictable—not by age or sex or occupation or location or dress or affluence or vocabulary or color or national origin. We tried, and we failed. It's all so very personal.

9. Reading expands rather than restricts. It raises the knowledge horizon rather than lowering it or merely maintaining the *status quo*. It is an addition, available for use or storage today, re-callable for reference tomorrow.

10. Our study says "Down with censorship." Its clear message: Let the young read whatever their individual needs say they ought to read. What we have found is the answer to people who want to censor books. It is not the books they censor at all, but the well-being of whatever audience they presume to be protecting.

———

What we learned from listening to America was that *all* reading is good, that *no one* else can predict what will make the greatest difference in any individual's life. Censors presume to know what difference a book will make to certain individuals, and this is the great flaw in their approach, for after this study, we *know* that this is an unrealistic presumption. No censor can foretell what will motivate the bored, inform the unknowing, inspire even the genius.

If any of us, youngsters on up, does not find the reading needed at the time needed, the damage can be irreparable.

What a shame that some of the citizens who represent all the rest of us on governing boards and school boards and library boards and county boards and city councils—what a shame that some of these people succumb to the threats, always emptier than the protagonists proclaim, of the censors.

Patricia and I went into this study with great enthusiasm for books and reading. Along the way, there were those who said to us the book is dead, slain by the new electronic delivery systems.

But our journey listening to America tells us that this simply is not so.

What will determine the future of the book is not a some*thing*, but a some*one*—or millions of someones who have found, or are still searching for, the books that make the difference.

APPENDIX

TITLES OF THE BOOKS THEY NAMED

Some interviewees named a type of book or subject
without specifying titles or author:

calorie counter, 70
cats, 78–79
comic books, 74–75
comparative religions, 69–70
computer language manual, 32
flying adventures, 79–80
Greek mythologies, 19
history, 46
how-to-do-it, 21

Abraham Lincoln, 94–95
love stories, 68
Nuremberg trial records, 61–62
biographies of General Pershing, 92–93
Margaret Sanger's biography, 96–97
the plays of Bernard Shaw, 28
science fiction, 69
union histories, 51–52
westerns, 96

Some defied categorization: "The book that wasn't there."
No title, no author—"never saw it but know what effect it had."

THE AUTHORS OF THOSE BOOKS

Abbey, Edward, *The Monkey Wrench Gang*, 50
Alcoholics Anonymous, *Alcoholics Anonymous*, 6
Alcott, Louisa M., *Little Women*, 91–92
Alger, Jr., Horatio, various, 95
Allen, John, ed., *One Hundred Great Lives* (Mary Derieux, author), 29
Aristotle, *Ethics*, 60; *Poetics*, 60
Austen, Jane, *Pride and Prejudice*, 94

Bach, George Robert, and Peter Wyden, *The Intimate Enemy: How to Fight Fair in Love and Marriage*, 98
Bach, Richard, *Jonathan Livingston Seagull*, 99
Barrett, William E., *Woman on Horseback*, 90–91
Bates, H. E., *Fair Stood the Wind for France*, 18–19
Baum, L. Frank, *The Wizard of Oz*, 84
Bellow, Saul, *Henderson the Rain King*, 15
Bok, Edward, *The Americanization of Edward Bok*, 77
Brontë, Emily, *Wuthering Heights*, 33
Brown, Claude, *Manchild in the Promised Land*, 54
Buber, Martin, *The Way of Man*, 20–21
Buscaglia, Leo, *Love*, 72

Carnegie, Dale, *How to Win Friends and Influence People*, 21
Cervantes, *Don Quixote*, 100–101

Coleman, John, *Blue Collar Journal: A College President's Sabbatical*, 15–17
Cousins, Norman, *Anatomy of an Illness*, 20
Cronin, A. J., *The Keys of the Kingdom*, 4
Curie, Eve, *Madame Curie: A Biography*, 22

Dickens, Charles, *David Copperfield*, 77
Dostoyevsky, *The Idiot*, 44
Douglass, Frederick, *Life and Times of Frederick Douglass*, 56–58
Doyle, Sir Arthur Conan, *Sherlock Holmes*, 99–100; *The White Company* (2 entries), 80, 83
Dumas, Alexandre (*fils*), *Camille*, 82
Dumas, Alexandre (*père*), *The Count of Monte Cristo*, 77
Durant, Will, *The Story of Philosophy*, 22–23
Dykeman, Wilma, *The Tall Woman*, 15

Eliot, George, *The Mill on the Floss*, 23–24
Ellison, Ralph, *Invisible Man*, 44
Emerson, Ralph Waldo, *Compensation*, 58–59; "The American Scholar," 61

Ferber, Edna, *Great Son*, 70–71
Ferlinghetti, Lawrence, *A Coney Island of the Mind*, 89–90
Field, Eugene, *The Poems of Eugene Field*, 81

108

Some interviewees named just the author—"anything by..."

Horatio Alger, Jr.

Emilie Loring

Roy Rogers and Dale Evans

Charles M. Russell

William Shakespeare

George Bernard Shaw

New York:
  Brooklyn, 12–13
  Buffalo, 52–53
  Jackson Heights, 72–73
  New Rochelle, 56–58
  New York (12), 10, 13–14, 28–29,
    29, 30, 54, 56, 62, 78–79, 79, 83,
    86–87
  Syracuse, 20–21
North Carolina:
  Chapel Hill, 27
  Charlotte, 98
  Cherokee (2), 14, 15
Ohio:
  Bellevue, 24–25
  Cincinnati, 70
  Columbus (2), 25–27, 58–59
  Westerville, 74–75
Oregon: Cottage Grove, 21
Pennsylvania:
  Pittsburgh, 65
  Swarthmore, 69
South Carolina: Fort Sumter National
    Monument, 61
South Dakota: Crazy Horse,
    98–99

Tennessee:
  Nashville (2), 30, 66
  Oak Ridge, 28
Texas:
  Dallas (3), 44, 50–51, 70
  Grapevine, 96
  Houston, 99
Utah:
  Logan (2), 23, 31–32
  Salt Lake City, 14
Vermont: Stowe, 63
Virginia:
  Blacksburg, 60
  Chatmoss, 53
  Chesapeake, 97–98
  Portsmouth, 53
  Richmond, 74
Washington:
  Seattle (6), 14, 15–17, 21, 60–61, 66,
    85–86
  Spokane (2), 19–20, 69
Wisconsin: Stevens Point, 72
Wyoming:
  Cheyenne (5), 9–10, 22, 34, 49–50, 60
  Horse Creek, 17
  Laramie, 44–45

THEIR OCCUPATIONS

actor—3 entries, 4, 10, 73
adult bookstore manager, 66
advertising writer, 54
airline pilot, 79–80
airline stewardess, 70
All Things Considered (NPR program)
    co-host, 45–46
architect, 51
artist ("Shoe" comic strip), 74
artist ("Terry and the Pirates," "Steve
    Canyon" comic strips), 32–33
artist (western paintings), 34
attorney—2 entries, 6–7, 34
author—11 entries, 12, 44, 46, 50–51,
    58, 64, 77, 83, 88–89, 90, 91
automobile assembly-line utility man, 59
automobile dealer, 74–75

beauty-parlor manager, 70
book dealer, 20
book publisher—4 entries, 30, 75–76,
    79, 95
book reporter and reviewer, newspaper,
    radio, and TV, 84–85

brewery line worker, 53–54
business executive, 15

Chicago White Sox former owner,
    80–81
command master chief, U.S. Navy
    submarine school, 77–78
Common Cause founder, 52
cooking teacher, 22–23
cosmetics firm executive, 69–70

dairy farmer, 50
Dallas Cowboys professional football
    linebacker, 70
dean, academic studies, Philadelphia
    College of Textiles & Science, 69
dean of geology and mines, University
    of Idaho, 61
dean of students, Wellesley College, 94

early American historical consultant,
    38–40
editor and writer, 7–8
English department chairman, 60

professor of political science, 30
psychologist, 23
publisher, Chase's Calendar of Annual
   Events, 89
Publishers Weekly executive editor,
   78–79

rabbi emeritus, 65
radio reporter, 52–53
radio, TV, and film director,
   archdiocese of Denver, 64
railroad worker, 14
ranch wife, 17
Ray of Hope founder, 66–68
real estate salesperson, 99
retired—2 entries, 53, 68

Saturday Review editor emeritus, 81–82
sculptor, 98–99
seaman, U. S. Navy, 99–100
secretary—2 entries, 15, 72–73
silver mine diamond driller, 51–52
silver mine operations manager, 45
silversmith, candlestick maker, 3
sociologist, 29–30
Southern Baptist Convention personal
   evangelism department head, 64

state education official, 100
state legislator, 49–50
state treasurer, 22
student—2 entries, 19–20, 23

talent agency staff member, 69
teacher—4 entries, 9–10, 14, 31–32, 59
truck driver, 97–98
tugboat skipper, 31
TV newsman—2 entries, 63, 86–87
TV writer, 56

U.S. Army general who became
   ambassador to France, then
   president, Arthur D. Little Company,
   92–93
U.S. district court judge, 99
university administrator—2 entries,
   18–19, 31–32
University Microfilms founder, 33–34

waiter at Riccardo's, Chicago, 100–101
waitress at Durgin-Park, Boston, 21
writer—3 entries, 12–13, 83, 94

yacht designer, 34–35
youth advocate, 41

THEIR NAMES

Wainwright, Margaret, Seattle,
Wash., 21
Walker, Margaret (Armstrong),
Jackson, Miss., 64
Waller, Mary, Los Angeles, Calif., 69
Welch, Michael, Hokah, Minn.,
53–54
Wentworth, Russ, Wichita, Kan.,
18–19
West, Dolores, Cherokee, N.C., 15
White, Nancy, Spokane, Wash., 69
Wiggins, J. Russell, Ellsworth, Maine,
87–88

Wilson, Jean, Boston, Mass., 21
Wong, Jade Snow, San Francisco,
Calif., 90
Wright, David, New York, N.Y., 54

Yon, Elizabeth, Chesapeake, Va.,
97–98

Zangermeister, John, Bellevue, Ohio,
24–25
Ziolkowski, Korczak, Crazy Horse,
S.D., 98–99

Plus 6 anonymous from:

Atlanta (2), Miami, Los Angeles,
San Francisco, Seattle

The text of this book was set in Plantin, a typeface cut in 1913 by The Monotype Corporation, London. Though the face bears the name of the great Christopher Plantin, who in the latter part of the sixteenth century owned, in Antwerp, the largest printing and publishing firm in Europe, it is a rather free adaptation of designs by Claude Garamond (c. 1480–1561) made for that firm. With its strong, simple lines, Plantin is a no-nonsense face of exceptional legibility.

Cover design and title page by Virginia Tan